"Getting Back to Basics practice. Karen Howard provides a solid theological and educational foundation for her religious education program, and writes in understandable language. She leads the reader through the step by step process she followed to redirect her parish program. A religious education program that serves the entire family is an excellent way to meet the formational and informational needs of children and adults. With the renewed emphasis on adult faith formation that we are now experiencing, *Getting Back to Basics* will make an excellent resource for a parish that is looking for ways to reach out to people of all ages."

Susan Abbott
Assistant Director for Family Catechesis
Office of Religious Education
Archdiocese of Boston

"Getting Back to Basics: A Parish Plan for Family Catechesis will help a parish community move toward the rewards of family catechesis. In the hectic lives of today's families, this program offers parents an opportunity to update their own understanding of the Catholic faith and then to discuss with other parents how parenting directly promotes their children's lives of faith. It also conveys to children a powerful message: that faith formation is a life-long process."

Rev. Joseph F. McGlone
Pastor, Corpus Christi Parish
Auburndale, MA

Getting Back to Basics

A
PARISH PLAN
FOR FAMILY
CATECHESIS

Karen L. Howard

TWENTY-THIRD PUBLICATIONS
A Division of Bayard   MYSTIC, CT 06355

Dedicated to

Father Joseph McGlone,
pastor of Corpus Christi,
and to all the wonderful parishioners
in that part of the kingdom!

Twenty-Third Publications
A Division of Bayard
185 Willow Street
P.O. Box 180
Mystic, CT 06355
(860) 536-2611
(800) 321-0411
www.twentythirdpublications.com

© Copyright 2001 Karen Howard, Ph.D. All rights reserved.
No part of this publication may be reproduced in any manner without prior
written permission of the publisher. Write to the Permissions Editor.

ISBN:1-58595-142-0
Library of Congress Catalog Card Number: 2001131616
Printed in the U.S.A.

Contents

A Parish Plan for Family Catechesis

Introduction

Spring of 1996 was a watershed time for Corpus Christi Parish in Newton, Massachusetts. That year, a new parish model of catechesis was introduced to the parishioners of the parish, located outside Boston. The previous year, the parish had undergone a visitation by the regional bishop, an event which occurs once every six years in the Boston archdiocese. Although all parish staff members knew the existing religious education program (based on the standard one-hour weekday class) was not working as well as it could, the problems really hit home with the visit of the regional bishop.

In this diocese, the customary procedure for the visitation is that the bishop be present and worship with parishioners at all the Masses. On the weekend of the bishop's visit, he had asked to visit two Sunday religious education classes, which were overflow classes from the regularly scheduled weekday classes. Each of the classes had between ten and twelve primary grade students in it. The bishop asked the children what they were studying and tried to engage them in conversation. When he asked how many had been to Mass that morning, he was astounded to learn that only one or two students in each class had been to Mass or were planning to attend Mass later that day. (The class times were situated between two Masses.) The bishop could not get over the fact that the students were already in the church building but would not be staying for Mass. His subsequent directive to the DRE and to the pastor was that they do whatever it took to have the children get back to attending Sunday liturgy on a regular basis.

The first thing the DRE did was to meet with the religious education advisory board to help study the problems with the existing religious education program, and begin to identify solutions.

This advisory board consisted of the DRE, her assistant, and four other parishioners, all of whom were parents.

During its first year, the board looked not only at the particular issues of the religious education program at Corpus Christi Parish, but at a broader scope of issues affecting religious education programs across the diocese and across the country. The board began to surmise that religious education was being relegated to the same status as scouting, hockey, or ballet lessons; that is, another activity to fill the children's time—and often, one that substituted for babysitting. For many people, the connection between religious education and Sunday liturgy had been lost.

In addition to the perception that religious education was just another thing to do, there were other factors influencing the way the program was regarded. In more and more families, both parents worked outside the home, and more and more households were being run by single parents. Children were going from school to aftercare programs to religious education classes, then back to the aftercare programs until Mom or Dad got home. Many of the parents were young couples who belonged to the generation of post-Vatican II experimentation with Catholic education, and who were not sure of their own religious knowledge. Many were also developing their own careers, and not only working but attending college. By the time the weekend came, they were exhausted.

This first year of study by the advisory board helped to identify many problems. It determined that the children were getting a bare minimum of teaching on the history and doctrine of the Catholic faith. Often, through no fault of their own, the children did not know how to put the teachings of their faith into practice or relate those teachings to liturgy. In addition, many families were not going to Mass. Parents were stressed. There was little faith sharing among children and parents; there was even less among parents in the parish. And while catechists tried to keep the lines of communication open between themselves and parents, more often than not, the catechists were viewed as the den mothers of religion classes and not taken very seriously. The advisory board discussed several approaches that might correct some of the concerns. It thought of shifting all the classes to Sunday, but the experience with the two overflow classes showed that this approach wouldn't be enough to ensure that children and their parents would attend Mass. The board even entertained the idea that there be no religious education classes for one year and instead, everyone asked to attend weekly Mass; but it quickly concluded that this would simply mean a year of vacation for many people.

The board looked at what was already in place in the religious education program that seemed to work well, such as community building activities that had been done in years past. It discussed the lure of special liturgical seasons—Advent, Christmas, Lent, and Easter—along with the power of the gospel message. It considered the spiritual hunger prevalent in our society, and how people look for nourishment in places other than the institutional church. It observed the committed families who were always there and who wanted more for their children and themselves.

The board examined lectionary-based programs versus regular curriculum programs. It discussed the *Catechism of the Catholic Church* and explored *Catechism*-based materials. It discussed the need for adult education and formation, especially for the parents. In the end, the board drafted a new model for religious education, one that would try to re-center Sunday within the life of the family. This model would encourage a vision of Sunday not only as a day of worship, but as a day of rest and relaxation as well as a day of learning and growing together.

The next few months proved crucial. The DRE and the advisory board took their findings to the pastor, the pastoral associate, and the parish pastoral council. After much discussion, it was decided that the model suggested by the board would be endorsed by all parties involved—the DRE, the religious education advisory board, the pastor, the pastoral associate, and the pastoral council—and then tried in the parish for one year. Thus, when the idea was presented to the parish at large, it was done not with a single voice but by the leadership of the entire parish.

Here follow the key elements in the model adopted by Corpus Christi Parish.

• The entire family would come together twice a month on Sundays for liturgy and education. At least one parent would be required to attend both Mass and a one-hour class that would follow the liturgy.

• The parish would adopt a lectionary-based curriculum, which would be cross-referenced to the *Catechism of the Catholic Church*.

• At each family liturgy, one class would have a special participatory role in the Mass.

• Twice a year, the Sunday classes for both parents and children would feature family projects where each family would work together as a team.

The religious education program would be expanded to include a preschool class for three and four year olds, as well as kindergarten classes. Children under three years old would be invited to stay with their parents during the parents' sessions.

The plan went as follows: parents were to attend Mass with their children and then come downstairs to the church hall. While the children went off to their classrooms, the parents would sit down at tables of eight to ten people that were set with coffee and pastries. Guest speakers would address the parents on the same lectionary theme that the children were learning about in their classrooms. By the end of the morning, both parents and children would have a common discussion topic for the week based on the gospel of the day.

It was decided that there would be no classes held on three-day or holiday weekends, and that there would be a month-long break from mid-December to mid-January. When there were no classes scheduled, families were encouraged to attend liturgy whenever and wherever it would be best for them. But on the days that classes met, however, the parish would have their undivided attention for two hours.

In the spring of 1996, as classes were coming to an end for the year, the new program for September was announced. The program was called "Retrieving the Sabbath," inspired by a lectionary reading from the Second Book of Chronicles (36:14–16, 19–23). The program was outlined at an informational parents meeting, including a summary of the work of the board and the parish leadership in developing this program. To support the rationale for the new model, most of the theological content for the meeting was taken from the *Catechism of the Catholic Church*, from the section on the third commandment. (The *Catechism* does a wonderful job of explaining the spirit of the law behind this commandment, to wit, that rest and re-creation of spirit go hand-in-hand with worshiping the Lord as a way of keeping holy the Sabbath.)

Due to obligations such as work schedules, a few parents had difficulty with the participatory requirement. Two provisions were made for those who absolutely could not come on Sundays. The first was that another family or family member would agree to pick up the children, take them to the sessions, stay with the children, and keep the parents informed as to what the children were learning. The other option was that parents could teach their children at home. In this case, the DRE would meet with the child and, if possible, the parents at regular intervals to determine if the lessons were being understood.

A few families could not come to terms with the new requirements and left the parish for other Catholic parishes. The vast majority, however, seemed to understand the intent of this new model of religious education and were willing to give it a try. The prospect of intergenerational learning also seemed to intrigue many. (During the introduction of this religion education program, it was helpful to learn that one of the local synagogues was also exploring intergenerational learning models.)

What followed the preliminary work (and what is still in place today) was a wonderful rebirth of the religious education program. Children and parents began to talk more about their Catholic faith. Parents began to meet other parents and have the time to share their faith concerns with each other. The twice-a-month schedule seemed acceptable to most families. Mass attendance significantly increased as did participation in the liturgy. Since the program provided speakers for the parents' educational sessions, and since many of the current catechists were these same parents, new non-parent catechists had to be recruited. Thus, a wide range of Corpus Christi's twenty-something parishioners, the single, engaged, or newly married couples, came forward and began to assist in catechizing. The family projects which were scheduled twice a year usually spilled over into other parish or home activities. Some of the family projects took on a broader dimension of outreach to the community. Parish liturgies became much more alive and celebratory.

After two actual years and three years of projected lectionary-based lessons, an evaluation of curriculum content was made. From this came a recommendation to include a short workbook on the *Catechism of the Catholic Church* along with the lectionary materials for each grade. The plan called for the catechists to spend ten minutes of each lesson on the workbook, which reviewed prayers and basics of the Catholic faith, then move on to the lectionary curriculum. The *Catechism* workbooks went home with the children after each class so that parents could help their daughters and sons review the material. This process helped encourage further religious education and dialogue at home on a very simple level.

Overall, "Retrieving the Sabbath" was not a panacea for the religious education problems that had concerned the parish. Not all problems were solved and not everyone was as excited about their faith and their family's faith development as the next one. What emerged with this family model of religious education, however, was a wonderful new way of restoring the connection between liturgy and religious education. Corpus Christi began to retrieve what was previously hidden: a vibrant community of knowledgeable and committed Catholic families, along with a renewed sense of the sacredness of the Sabbath experience.

What follows in this book is a description of the theological foundations and the educational theories for this model along with all the necessary "how-to's." Step-by-step directions are given to demonstrate how to begin the program, keep the lines of communication open, design the curriculum, and add any necessary components to the basic curriculum, as well as ways to put evaluation mechanisms into place for critiquing and further development. Four appendices feature 1) a sample year of lectionary-based catechesis; 2) suggested resources; 3) sample letters, bulletin announcements, and meeting agendas; and 4) ideas for project Sundays.

Since Corpus Christi Parish began using this model in 1997, the bishops of the United States have written a landmark document on religious education, titled "Our Hearts Were Burning Within Us." In this document, the bishops call all religious educators to place more of an emphasis on the catechesis of adults, while still addressing the catechetical needs of children. Family programs, or intergenerational learning, are one of the ways in which the bishops see this becoming more of a reality.

In writing this book, my hope is that this model of family catechesis may serve to enrich the church at large and assist families in sharing their faith with one another.

Chapter 1

Laying the Foundation

In Matthew's gospel, the followers of Jesus are given a mandate: "Go therefore and make disciples of all nations, baptizing them in the name of the Father and of the Son and of the Holy Spirit and teaching them to obey everything that I have commanded you. And remember, I am with you always, to the end of the age" (Mt 28:19–20). So begins the work of Christian catechesis.

From the earliest written accounts of catechesis, eucharistic worship was incorporated into the initiation and education of the followers of Jesus. In the *Didache*, written toward the end of the first century CE and sometimes called *The Teaching of the Twelve Apostles*, we find these words: "On the Lord's own day, assemble in common to break bread and offer thanks." Ignatius of Antioch later linked the Jewish Sabbath observances, based in the Hebrew Scriptures, to the Christian Sunday observances, now based and expressed as part of Christ's passover and resurrection.

In *The New Dictionary of Theology*, Shawn Madigan traces the early development of Sunday in the Christian tradition. She relates that Sundays became "little Easters" for believers as they strove to remember and celebrate the Paschal mysteries. In the early Christian communities, "Sunday" was known by many names. The Roman term "sun's day" was given a Christian meaning as early as the second century when Christians began to call Christ their "Sun," for he had risen anew on Easter. Sabbath observances for the Jews had defined the Lord's day as the last day of the week, the seventh day, upon which God rested after creation. Christ became Lord for his disciples, so by the end of the first century, the Lord's day had become known as Christ's day. Early Christians also called Sunday "the eighth day," the day that followed the day of rest and symbolized the newness of creation in the aftermath of the resurrection.

Irenaeus of Lyons extended the work of catechesis to cover the entire panorama of salvation history, from Genesis forward, when he acknowledged that the Christian faith was forever linked to its Hebrew roots. For Irenaeus, the followers of Christ were not only to learn the story of God's salvific love throughout history; they were to be immersed in the Sabbath, "to constantly keep the Sabbath, giving homage to God in the temple of God which is man's body." The Jewish perception of Sabbath was to acknowledge God's rest after creation, and to enter into that rest in order to delight in the Lord. But it was not until 321 CE that the emperor Constantine limited the amount of work that Christians were allowed to do on Sundays. (Centuries later, Thomas Aquinas later reminded the church that the purpose of this limitation was to delight in the Lord.)

The third commandment, found in the Exodus story, first directed believers to keep holy the Sabbath. Today, the *Catechism of the Catholic Church* provides a wonderful synthesis of the complexities of that command. It demonstrates how the Sabbath is to provide us with rest and refreshment as well as give worship to God within the context of the Eucharist. The *Catechism* states:

> The celebration of Sunday observes the moral commandment inscribed by nature in the human heart to render to God an outward, visible, public, and regular worship "as a sign of his universal beneficence to all."(#2176)

> The Sunday celebration of the Lord's Day and his Eucharist is at the heart of the Church's life. "Sunday is the day on which the Pascal mystery is celebrated in light of the apos-

tolic tradition and is to be observed as the foremost holy
day of obligation in the universal Church." (#2177)

Just as God "rested on the seventh day from all his work
which he had done," human life has a rhythm of work
and rest. The institution of the Lord's day helps everyone
enjoy adequate rest and leisure to cultivate their familial,
cultural, social, and religious lives. (#2184)

So the purpose of the Sabbath is really twofold: to provide rest
and re-creation of spirit for humanity, and to draw humanity to
worship around the table of the Lord so that we may delight in
him. The *Catechism* goes so far as to call all Christians to work
together to seek recognition of Sundays as a legal holiday, thereby
giving a public example of prayer, respect, and joy while defending
the contributions of the Christian tradition to the spiritual life of
society (#2188). Sundays should be days set aside to worship and
to rest, to re-create one's spirit, and to regroup as family and as
community. The letter to the Hebrews hints at this supportive
dimension as well: "And let us consider how to provoke one
another to love and good deeds, not neglecting to meet together,
as is the habit of some, but encouraging one another, and all the
more as you see the Day approaching" (Hb 10:24–25).

But how does observance of the Sabbath intersect with catechesis today? The new *General Directory for Catechesis* (GDC)
states that the functions and forms of the eucharistic celebration
are linked to the work of catechesis when they call people
together and call them to faith:

This function is the most immediate expression of the
missionary mandate of Jesus. It is realized through the
"primary proclamation"....The religious awakening of the
children of Christian families is also an eminent form of
this function. (#51)

Once the gospel is proclaimed and families are awakened to the faith, the ministry of the word uses various forms to continue education in the faith. By forms, the *GDC* refers to the many ways in which the word is broken open for believers. Some forms are apart from Sunday celebrations, such as Scripture study, theological instruction, or a Christian reading of life events. Others are intimately connected to Sunday worship celebrations, such as liturgical catechesis, which strives to prepare parishioners for the sacraments by promoting "a deeper understanding and experience of the liturgy," and "must be regarded as an eminent kind of catechesis" (#71).

The Liturgy of the Word is not the only part of Sunday liturgy that catechizes and nourishes the believer:

> In the Christian community, the disciples of Jesus Christ are nourished at a twofold table: "that of the word of God and that of the Body of Christ." The Gospel and the Eucharist are the constant food for the journey to the Father's House. (#70)

So it is the entire Sabbath experience, including rest and re-creation of both body and spirit, and the celebration of Eucharist, that is caught up in the work of catechesis. Everyone who gathers around the table helps to refresh and renew one another as we engage in worship together. The sweetness of the word and of the body of Christ enables and nourishes those it touches. Every parishioner makes Sabbath for one another as each allows the spirit of faith within themselves to recognize the holy, to delight in the Holy One, and to reverence one another.

The word "catechesis" comes from the Greek and means to teach by word of mouth, to echo, in a sense, especially one's faith experience. Catholic Christians have always endeavored to share their faith experience of the risen Christ with each other, but especially with their children. Parents today continue to do so, many because they themselves have a vibrant, passionate relationship with Christ. Others see their faith in Jesus Christ, his church, and his teachings as a way of passing along some of their most treasured values. Others may not be so sure of their own faith and understanding about Jesus Christ and his church; they just know they want their children to hear and know about God. Still others seem to be convinced that handing on the faith is the right thing to do, that it is part of their job as parents, even though they are not too sure about their own beliefs.

Intergenerational learning
In recent years, the whole concept of family has been redefined, with single-parent households, adoptive families, grandparents raising grandchildren, and many mixed families of stepmoms and stepdads working alongside moms and dads in raising their children. The high rate of divorce and remarriage has resulted in cases of joint custody, and many children often split their weekends between parents. Complicating matters even more is the broad range in the age of today's parents of school-age children. The usual group in their twenties and thirties are now joined by parents in their forties, fifties, and even sixties. Thus, the cognitive, moral, and spiritual development of parents, on the whole, is at many different stages.

A common theme throughout many of the catechetical documents written in the wake of Vatican II is that parents are the primary educators of their children. Many pastors and DREs have belabored this directive in order to increase parent participation and responsibility in religious education. There is another side to this directive, however. At baptism, parents bring their children to the doors of the parish so that they may be welcomed into the Christian community, and so that the parents might be supported by the entire community in the process of catechesis. Thus, the adage, "it takes a village to raise a child" has never been more true than within the role of the faith community in catechesis.

It is at the Sunday eucharistic celebration that ordinary Catholic believers join their voices and hearts and lives in a common liturgical purpose, that is, giving thanks and praise to God. It is at these same celebrations that professing, believing Catholics most effectively engage in the work of catechesis. Thus, the whole worshiping community needs to take an active role in the process of catechesis in the parish. Religious education is not meant only to instruct the young; it is meant to sustain all believers. It is a lifelong venture.

If we see catechesis as a process involving the whole parish community, this will naturally lead to an understanding of religious education as an intergenerational endeavor. Working with Catholics of all ages is an absolutely fascinating and exhilarating experience. But first, there are some ground rules that must be laid down in order for things to go smoothly.

Rule one: *No one starts at the same level.*
Levels of cognitive ability, as well as emotional and social development, will be radically different with an intergenerational model. Erik Erikson has been lauded as a pioneer in the study of life cycles since 1950, when he published his groundbreaking work, *Childhood and Society*. He maintains that human beings move through stages of psychosocial development and toward generative adulthood as they move through the successful resolution of life's crises. Erikson cites the following eight stages in this development:

Birth to 12-18 months	basic trust vs. mistrust
12-18 months to 3 years	autonomy vs. shame or doubt (independence)
3 to 6 years	initiative vs. guilt (willing to try new things)
6 years to puberty	industry vs. inferiority (self-esteem and confidence)

Puberty to young adulthood	identity vs. role confusion (one's sense of self)
Young adulthood	intimacy vs. isolation (balance between self/others)
Middle adulthood	generativity vs. stagnation (guiding next generation)
Late adulthood	basic integrity vs. basic despair (acceptance of one's own life/death)

Daniel Levinson sees similar parallels of growth when he describes life as a series of journeys that move through the seasons of life to death. In his book *Seasons of a Man's Life*, he describes four seasons of roughly twenty years apiece: childhood and adolescence, early adulthood, middle adulthood, and late adulthood. Levinson writes that each season has its own distinctive character, different from those that precede it and follow it. Each life season also has numerous elements, comparable to seasons of the year (spring, summer, fall, winter) or seasons of a day (morning, afternoon, and evening) or seasons of love, war, or illness. According to this theory, imagery plays an important role in connecting the seasons.

Rule two: *Everyone learns differently.*
In 1952, a Swiss biologist named Jean Piaget outlined several stages in cognitive development. From this, he formulated a theory that intelligence is acquired in an orderly sequence, closely related to age:

Sensorimotor stage (birth to 2 years): the infant changes from a being who responds primarily through reflexes to one who can organize activities in relation to the environment.

Preoperational stage (two to seven years): the child develops a representational system and uses symbols, such as words, to represent people, places, and events.

Concrete operational stage (seven to twelve years): the child can solve problems logically if the problems are focused on the here and now.

Formal operational stage (twelve years to adult): The person can think in abstract terms and deal with hypothetical situations.

Lawrence Kohlberg furthers the formal operation theories of Piaget and the work of Erikson when he adds stages of moral development to the mixture. He links stages of moral reasoning with stages of intellectual development. The complexities of behavior and ethics are tied to one's intellectual growth and age:

Level 1

Stage 1 (ages 4-10): punishment and obedience

Stage 2 (ages 4-10): instrumental purpose and exchange (you scratch my back, I'll scratch yours)

Level 2

Stage 3 (ages 10-13): maintaining mutual relations (the golden rule)

Stage 4 (ages 10-13): social systems and conscience formation

Level 3

Stage 5 (ages 13, young adult or never): morality of contract of individual rights

Stage 6 (ages 13, young adult or never): morality of contract of universal ethical principles

Carol Gilligan, a colleague of Lawrence Kohlberg at Harvard, elaborates on yet another aspect of moral development; that is, the difference between men's and women's voices. In her book *In a Different Voice: Psychological Theory and Women's Development*, Gilligan posits that women learn differently from men. She also writes that women arrive at moral decisions and actions differently from men. According to Gilligan, women use the sense of hearing far more than their male counterparts, who generally use the sense of sight in learning. Since in using the sense of hearing women must therefore be listening to someone, their moral actions often come out of relationships rather than objective abstractions.

Rule three: *Everyone develops their relationship with God differently.* James Fowler builds upon all of the theories noted here with the stages of faith development found in his book *Becoming Adult, Becoming Christian.* Fowler identifies normal spiritual growth with normal developmental stages in human life, and categorizes them into seven levels:

Primal (0-2 years). One learns basic trust, is introduced to intimacy with others, and begins to perceive one's primary caregivers as having superordinate power and wisdom, as well as perceive one's own dependence. Later these initial experiences of nurturing paternity and maternity will serve as images of God.

Intuitive-projective (2-6 years). Children begin to experiment with perception, feelings, and imagination as they try to construct a worldview, and often use religious symbols if they have been introduced.

Mythic-literal (7-12 years). Faith of this child relies on the narrative, rules, and implicit values (including religious values) of the family and community to engage in concrete operational thinking.

Synthetic-conventional (13-16 years). Early adolescent faith begins to see a breakdown in moral reciprocity, and the God of moral reciprocity dies and must be replaced; imagination and intelligence join forces to uncover interiority, both of self and of others, and previously held worldviews now become synthesized with interiority; the child cannot yet examine religious principles objectively.

Individuative-reflective (early adult to mid-life). Faith life is occasioned by a variety of experiences which cause the person to objectify, examine, and make critical choices about one's identity and one's beliefs; many adults never move past this stage.

Conjunctive (mid-life). Starts to see more to the self than the conscious ego, attempts to hold together various polarizations in life, e.g., rich and poor, young and old, darkness and light, masculine and feminine, etc. It proceeds to cherish paradoxes.

Universalizing (later life). Movement of a radical decentralization from self; faith calls the individual to begin to engage in a *kenosis,* or a self-emptying, and see beyond the self as the sole valuational reference point for worldview construction.

If we examine the lives of mystics or saints under fire, we often see a collapsing of Fowler's levels of spiritual growth, one upon another. For the ordinary process of catechesis, however, they provide a valuable guide and framework.

Rule four: *Everyone understands differently.*
According to St. Anselm, the definition of theology is "faith seeking understanding." Thus, we must add one more component to the educational mix if we seek understanding. There is a renewed interest today in the theory of multiple intelligences,

first put forth by Howard Gardner some fifteen years ago. Gardner suggests that every human being has several means of intelligence through which he or she may arrive at understanding. Schools have traditionally used only two: verbal intelligence and mathematical, or logic, intelligence. But there are at least six other intelligences: music, spatial, bodily or kinesthetic, interpersonal, intrapersonal, and naturalist. (Daniel Goleman has, of late, written about a ninth intelligence, emotional.)

Let's put this theory into the realm of religious education. One may learn to understand a concept of faith or theology more through the intelligence of music and ritual than through a textbook. Or, one may learn an understanding of the relationship between God and God's people through spatial arrangements rather than through Socratic questions and answers. When designing a program of intergenerational learning, it is helpful to be familiar with these rules and theories. More important, we must be willing to experiment with balance. If we are addressing a few hundred people of numerous ages and life experiences, we may have to use multiple mediums of communication.

In our lectionary-based program at Corpus Christi, we rely heavily on a multifaceted approach to intergenerational learning. First, we identify the core principle in each lesson. From there, we experiment with various mediums related to intelligences, stages, and seasons, to help break open the word. We have found that the more mediums used and the more they are held in balance with one another, the more the faith community will be able to learn and understand.

In order to address the different needs and learning styles in a parish, the DRE and the parish leadership need to become effective listeners. If a parish is engaged in family catechesis, the leadership must listen not only to the numerous voices in the pews, but to the dynamics of the families themselves. In a recent article in *Momentum* (February-March 2000), Peter Ilg cautions: "The emotional, physical, social and spiritual cohesiveness of family, more than anything else, determines the success or failure of religious education." He also maintains that the "family is a dynamic and developing system whose members are interdependent."

Members of a family, no matter what its configuration, are always in a growth pattern. In any given family, each of the individuals is different in some way or another from one year to the next. Especially with children, the space of a year may mean a new stage of development or new levels of awareness. The relationships among siblings and between children and parents are also changing as each grows into new stages and seasons. Those who are responsible for catechetics should not be afraid of the complexities of family dynamics, but rather relish them, for they too are tools for breaking open the core principles of the faith. Indeed, attentiveness to family dynamics can allow and assist parish catechesis to flourish.

Even if the DRE and parish leadership are dynamos at listening and attentiveness, however, they must not forget prayer in their discernment and planning. Prayer, reflection, and contemplation give birth to the energy behind catechesis, that is, to the driving force of the Holy Spirit. When the year has been outlined, the texts researched, the dynamics considered, and the mediums evaluated, step back to reflect and pray for guidance. Catechesis is the echoing of our faith experience of the risen Christ. If we want to tap into this faith experience, it is imperative that all members of catechetical leadership "Be still, and know that I am God!" (Ps 46:10), and allow the risen Christ a voice in his Spirit.

A shift in methodology
Since the Second Vatican Council, catechesis has undergone many changes. Most religious education programs, however, have settled on a methodology that begins with shared Christian

praxis. In this approach, narratives are employed about ordinary life experiences and discussion of those life experiences leads to sharing. Catholic Christian teaching is introduced and inserted into the story. From there, students are led to see the connections between ordinary life experiences, the doctrines of our faith, and the gospel.

While this may be a wonderful way to connect ordinary life to the gospel message, what I have observed over the past thirty years is that, more often that not, what is most remembered are the stories and *not* the teachings. Thus, we now have a whole generation of parents who know that God is love and who remember the stories they heard as children. But they are ill-prepared to articulate what it means to be a Catholic. There is an unparalleled power in the word of God, and a recent experience that I had with a catechumen may help to illustrate this point. During one of the Rites of Scrutiny, she became so overwhelmed by the words of Scripture and the rituals that went along with the words that she almost passed out. Afterwards, she revealed how overpowering the experience had been and how shocked she had been to find herself reacting in such a manner. She said it was as if "the Spirit took over."

The words of Scripture have power themselves, for the Word among us is the very center of catechesis. It was from this conviction that the catechetical leadership at Corpus Christi chose a lectionary-based model from which to proceed. Lessons are constructed around specific lectionary themes and then cross-referenced to the *Catechism of the Catholic Church*. One of the most significant distinctions in this methodology from the graded approach of the standard religious ed curriculum is that it allows everyone—no matter what level, stage, season, or intelligence—to all be on the same page.

For family catechesis to work, it is important that all members of the family have a common topic that they can learn and discuss and absorb together. The standard religious education curriculum simply does not allow this. For instance, if a family has a first grader, a fourth grader, and a sixth grader, one day's lesson might cover the goodness of creation in the first grade, a study of the second commandment in the fourth grade, and Paul's journey to Corinth in the sixth. And this does not take into account what the parents might be attempting to learn!

But consider what might happen if on any given Sunday, the religious education program asked the entire family to look at the story of the man born blind found in John 9:1–41. When we cross-reference this passage to the *Catechism* (#575, 588, 595, 596, 1151, 1504, 2173, and 2827), we find a wealth of material available to unpack the gospel, from calling sinners to repentance, to signs and symbols of healing, to the faith of believers, to the proper use of the Sabbath. Each member of the family might then begin to look at different elements of the story; the first grader could learn about healing, the fourth grader examine repentance, the sixth grader explore the faith of the sick, and the parents consider the use of Sabbath. When that family goes home from church that day, they have a common topic of faith for further discussion and implementation. They have learned in collaboration with each other, they have echoed their faith back to one another, and they have started to retrieve the Sabbath. They have also engaged in Jesus' mandate to go forth and teach, perhaps having realized the second part of that mandate: "And remember, I am with you always, until the end of the age" (Mt 28:20).

The risen Christ is with us always, in the work of mission and catechesis, until the end of the age. Let's look now at how we might build a program to spread the good news of Jesus along with the teachings of the Catholic church.

Chapter 2

How to Begin

Step one: Identify yourself and your needs

Before you begin work on developing a new model in catechesis, take a good look at your current model. Try to determine its strengths and its weaknesses. If you are interested in a family model of religious education, one that uses an intergenerational approach and more closely links catechesis to Sunday liturgy, you first need to ask yourself "why." What has led you to the conclusion that a change is needed, that more parent participation is needed or that the generations need to mix? Models in teaching or in catechesis are not changed easily. Are you at a crisis point, or do you simply want to do better? Do you have enough support for a change? The more you understand and articulate your present situation along with your hopes and dreams, the better equipped you will be to make changes in your catechetical program. Don't be afraid to dream a little, to reach for the stars.

Your initial work should be done with other key members of the parish, for example, the parish council, the religious education advisory board, the pastor, the parish staff, other catechists, and parents. It is critical that your pastor and the parish staff share your concerns and support your vision. Listen to one another. Together, begin to paint a picture of the ideal catechetical program. Doodle a little, sketch a little, fantasize a little, and then share your dreams with one another.

After this initial dreaming and sharing, it is usually helpful to take some time to reflect and pray about what you have outlined and discovered. Let the dreams of your first meeting(s) sink in. Make room for the Spirit. After the initial meetings, and for the bulk of the work, you will need to work with one committee or commission. A religious education advisory board is ideal for this part of the process.

If your parish does not have an advisory board, perhaps now is the time to start one. Oftentimes parishioners will come forward to help with a specific task, or if they can be given an anticipated timeline for a particular project. More importantly, it is very helpful to have the advice, knowledge, and experience of concerned parties from the parish in discussing your catechetical program. Assume that any board in existence or coming into existence for the purpose of redesigning a program will need to stay together for at least two years. The first year will be used to gather data, analyze it, explore options, and then propose the new program. The work of the second year will be in implementing the program and in making an initial and ongoing evaluation of it during the course of the first year.

Step two: Analyze your current situation
A few weeks after your initial listening sessions, gather all your information together and bring it to your committee or commission for a second meeting or set of meetings, and start to analyze your current program. Ask questions such as, what is not working in the present program? What do you want to see improved? You might want to write both questions and answers down on paper and post the paper in a place where people can easily see it. This can help everyone become more aware of how the process will work.

Look at the most positive aspects of your current program. You may want to keep these elements or incorporate them into a new model. For example, perhaps you have a really great first communion program. What works in that program? Parents are usually willing to do handsprings when their child is preparing to receive first communion. Preparation for first communion has a natural link to Sunday liturgy, and if the parents have not been regular churchgoers, they may even begin to attend Mass each week. Try to analyze parents' motivation. Why are they willing to do so much to ensure their child's first reception of the Eucharist? Observe the excitability and wonder of the children during this time. Is there a way to extend those feelings throughout the years of their religious education in the parish?

Perhaps another positive aspect of your program is the social outreach projects that seem to get families so energized. The Christmas "giving tree," food collections for local pantries, visits to nursing homes, and other such projects can often motivate students and parents alike to get more involved in the religious education program. Perhaps the Advent and Christmas season really pulls your families together. Perhaps the families regroup again for Lent and Easter, as weekend liturgies and even daily Mass become more important during these special times. What can the rituals and liturgical experiences of the church year contribute to catechesis in your parish? Pause to reflect and pray again.

Step three: Explore, gather, and propose
Now is the time to gather your group together for a third set of meetings to discuss what you have learned so far. Examine some of the problems that have surfaced and play with some possible solutions. Do more dreaming and wishing and exploring. Push the boundaries. Invent the scenarios. Walk through some possible proposals; would they have pastoral support? Can your facilities handle everyone meeting for religious education classes at the same time or must groups be broken down? Can you implement the new model all at once or will it need to be done over a few years? Will you need to run the graded program simulta-

neously for a while? Are your dreams attainable? What needs to be done in order for at least some of those dreams to become a reality? Map out a possible strategy.

Now may be the time to go back and get more input from others in the parish. What have the staff members said about the current religious education program? What do they think needs to be improved? Suggest your proposals to them. What are their concerns? Remember, pastors and other parish staff members are already busy. Respect their time constraints. Most are very willing, however, to dream with you as well as make some concrete suggestions. Value their collective years of experience in parish ministry.

If you have not done so already, gather a group of interested parents for a one-time meeting. What are their concerns? How do they want the religious education program to improve? Discuss the time constraints of today's modern families. Explore possible ways to use time more effectively, to enrich parish life, and to build community, along with ideas on how to improve religious education. Many of these areas are linked together in a parish; one feeds and supports the other.

Consider tapping into the resources available through the local school system. Often, valuable connections can be found between the principal's office or the guidance office and the parish religious education office which will support the religious education program and, at the same time, keep parishes aware of local school issues. There also may be opportunities for ecumenical or interfaith collaboration with the local schools. Many parents are already involved in their children's school programs, and often, there are parish members who are also involved in the local school system. Listen to those voices and use them.

When you have heard all the voices, it is time to return for a fourth meeting to play with ideas and to start the selection process. Prioritize the recommendations. Write them down. Which are similar? Can any be grouped together? Which recommendation is most important? Which one is next important? Select the three or four ideas that are most important and categorize them. Let's say your top priority is to improve family attendance at Sunday liturgy, the next is to increase parent education, and the third is improving the education of children. You can begin to strategize from those directives, balance them, and design a new program of religious education.

A good dose of common sense is useful at this stage. You are attempting to balance the new priorities you have just articulated with various learning styles, cognitive stages, and moral levels. Also, it is important to remember the time constraints of everyone involved. If you have to err on the side of any one particular group, do so on the side of the parents. These folks have the least amount of time and usually the most responsibilities. Do whatever you can to make it easier for them. In the program at Corpus Christi, for instance, refreshments, set-up, and various materials are always prepared ahead of time for parents. No classes are scheduled on holiday weekends, there is extra time off before Christmas, and family projects are incorporated into the regular Sunday sessions. Parent involvement is key in this type of program, so make it inviting whenever possible.

When you have your priorities articulated and written down, map out the year with a sample calendar which includes those priorities. Then begin to design your basic curriculum. What are the necessary components in your curriculum? For instance, if you have decided to employ a lectionary-based program, how will you ensure that prayer will be taught or that specific Catholic teachings will be incorporated into the program? If you want to use an intergenerational model, what type of curriculum will give you the same subject matter for any given level, be it preschool, sixth grade, or parents? (Chapters three and four will address these issues in more depth.)

When this part of the process is completed, you will need to obtain the approval of the pastor, the parish staff, and the parish council. If the pastor has not been involved in the planning process to this point, it is time to bring him in. Perhaps an entire book could be written on the need for effective communication between a DRE and the pastor in any given parish. Suffice it to say here that they need to listen to one another, respect each other's time, gifts, and perspectives, and go out of their way to talk with each other. Both pastor and DRE are to be about the business of service. Sometimes this takes place at a regular staff meeting, but often there isn't enough time at that meeting for discussing religious education in depth. If the staff meeting is your main vehicle of communication with the pastor, however, make sure religious education has a specific place on each meeting's agenda, time for you to provide an update or progress report to the pastor and the staff.

Some pastors set aside a regular time to meet with their DRE. I knew of one pastor who met every Friday afternoon after lunch with his DRE for one or two hours. It was his way of acknowledging how central religious education is to the life of the parish. Some pastors regularly eat lunch with their DRE and parish staff. This regularity provides ample time to update one another about the progress of a changing program or parish needs. Other pastors prefer to meet only when the DRE requests such a meeting. If this is the case in your parish, and if you are in the discernment process for redesigning a religious education program, you should meet with the pastor at least once a month.

The next group with whom you need to keep open communication is the rest of the parish staff. Religious education is central to most parishes, and it impacts numerous other programs and ministries within the parish. If you are suggesting a change, it is prudent not only to keep other staff members informed, but as was said earlier, to invite their input as well. This would include any other priests assigned to the parish, pastoral associates, youth ministers, secretaries, and even those who maintain the buildings and grounds, as a fundamental shift in religious education can impact their jobs as well. This sharing of information can happen at staff meetings, at lunch, or whenever staff gathers regularly. If there is no regular meeting time that you can tap into, it will be up to the DRE to seek out individual staff members and set aside some time to speak with them about the discernment process and proposed program. Know too that sometimes, written monthly updates can suffice.

Parish councils need to be brought on board early in this process as well. In many parishes, the DRE is a regular member of the council; if he or she is not, he or she will have to start attending some of these meetings and make sure that some time is regularly set aside for religious education updates. Most parish councils are very interested in their catechetical programs and if there is a discernment process and a fundamental shift being discussed, they will want to participate. One caution, however: you can gather data from the parish council and ask for their input, but it will be primarily the task of the DRE and his or her advisory board or commission to do the gathering, analyzing, and planning. Again, it is a question of listening to one another, balancing the voices, and letting each person or group address their specific tasks.

After the parish council is on board, it is up to the DRE and her or his religious education advisory board to assume the role of leadership in implementing any change in the religious education program. Parishes are made up of hundreds, sometimes thousands of voices. If you have listened well to a sample of the all the voices, then you should have enough feedback to launch a new program or a new direction in catechesis. The DRE—in some parishes, along with the religious education advisory board—has been commissioned by the pastor, and he by the bishop, with the task of religious education. Respect that role.

Implementation begins with strategies in communication. At this point, further input should be put on hold until after the new program has been tried and evaluated.

Step four: Strategies in communication
The DRE will have to communicate with various groups if there is to be a fundamental change in the direction of a religious education program. The one group that can assist the DRE with this task will be the religious education commission or advisory board.

If the DRE has been including the catechists in the discernment process, they will be aware of the coming changes. If not, regular communication needs to begin with this group. Start by scheduling a few initial meetings with them to prepare them for any changes that are anticipated. With this new direction in catechesis, you may find that several new catechists need to be recruited. In the traditional school model of catechesis, oftentimes the majority of catechists are parents. If your goal is to incorporate family catechesis into the parish program, parents will need to be on the other side of the desk, so to speak. They cannot be the catechists as well as the students.

As I mentioned in the Introduction, some of the young single adults and newly married adults in the parish came forward when we found that we needed more catechists at Corpus Christi. This twenty-something age group often gets lost in parish programs. But in this parish, we found that the need for catechists gave them a real entrée into the life of the parish, and they have enriched the religious education program beyond measure. Sometimes, senior parishioners will step forward to act as catechists, as well. Those whose families are already grown bring a wealth of practical experience to the art of passing on the faith. If you find that you will need a number of new catechists for the coming school year, you might want to begin your recruitment efforts in late spring or early summer, prior to putting the new program into place. This will allow plenty of time to orient both new and returning catechists on the particulars of your new program, and do some teacher training.

The next step in communication is to inform the parents that there will be a basic shift in the direction of the catechetical programs, and that this shift will require their participation and presence on a regular basis. This is the time to marshal your forces and present the new program to the parents from *all* the parish leadership, not just from the DRE or from the pastor. Be forewarned: there may be resistance. Prepare for it. Be ready to tell the parents why the current program is not working as well as you would like, and what you hope to accomplish by moving in a new direction. Outline the highlights of what has been done with regard to planning, study, and analysis, and provide a rationale for your decision. Emphasize that this process has the support and commitment of the parish leadership to try a new approach for one year.

If you decide to let parents know about the changes through a letter, try to include as many signatures of parish leaders as possible. Key signatures to have would be those of the DRE, the pastor, parish staff members, religious education advisory board members, and parish council members. Describe the changes briefly (see the sample letter in the appendices) and invite parents to an informational meeting.

The initial meeting can be chaired by the DRE and the pastor. In parishes with larger staffs, more voices lend more credibility. Those meetings can be chaired by the DRE, but the pastor, the deacon, the pastoral associate, the youth minister, or a religious education board member can all have a part. Remember, the more parish leaders the parents hear and see as being involved in the process, the easier it will be for them to understand why a new direction in catechesis is so important. If parents are told why a change is needed, that this direction initially will be tried for one year, and that this has the support of the parish leadership, they will be more open to hearing about any new process of catechesis. Change is often not easy and changing something as fundamental as a model in catechesis can be unnerving for some. In actuality, it will take at least one year before parents can fully realize all that can be gained from family-based catechesis.

You will find sample meeting agendas in the appendices. Ideally, you will want to schedule these meetings for late spring, near the end of the academic year, when parents and families are still around. During the summer, too many folks are on vacation. Telling people ahead of time about a new religious education program gives parents more time to reflect on the changes and make room in their schedules for the new requirements.

After informing the parents, it is time to announce the change to the parish at large. This is a great opportunity to educate the whole parish about its role as a faith community in the work of catechesis. When a family brings forward a candidate for baptism, they ask the entire church for entrance to the faith community. And so it is this entire church that is called upon to respond to help in faith formation. This is an opportunity to remind each parishioner that catechesis is the responsibility of all parishioners and that this new direction will require the participation of as many people as possible.

A sample timetable

Now that we've talked about about what to do to begin the process, here is a way to go about it. To work most effectively for a change in the direction of catechesis, especially if you want to link catechesis to Sunday liturgy and a renewed observance of the Sabbath, you must take the time and care to do the task well.

While ideas for change may have been percolating for some time, the actual discernment process can be accomplished during one academic year. As described above, there are four basic steps for this year of analysis and proposal:

1. identify current realities and dream of the future,
2. analyze the current program;
3. a) explore new ideas, listen to voices, propose;
     b) make selections, prioritize, design curriculum;
4. strategize for communication.

Four sets of meetings can be held to cover the first three steps. At the first meeting, plan to identify the issues and dream for the future. At the second meeting, analyze the current program, looking at both positive and negative aspects. For the third meeting, explore ideas, listen to the various voices from the parish, and make proposals. Finally, at the fourth meeting, you should be ready to make selections, prioritize issues and concerns, and design a curriculum. After your first four meetings (or sets of meetings, if you find that more than one is necessary for each step), you can begin to develop strategies for communication with the various groups mentioned earlier in this chapter.

Generally, each step of the process will take about two months, so that a timeline might look like this:

First meeting (September/October)
- *Identify and dream.*

Second meeting (November/December)
- *Analyze the current program.*

Third meeting (January/February)
- *Explore ideas, listen to voices, propose.*

Fourth meeting (March/April)
- *Make selections, prioritize, design curriculum.*

Post-meetings (April/May)
- *Develop communication strategies.*

It cannot be stressed enough how important it is for all parties involved to know by the end of the academic year that there will be substantial changes coming in the following year. Spring is the time for planting new seeds, and in order for your catechetical program to flourish and bear fruit, you must plant wisely. Give everyone ample time to reflect and pray about the changes. Let summer be an opportunity to nourish the ground that you have laid for your new program. Then, in the fall and winter, when the harvest has been collected and stored, the books have been bought and the classes have been scheduled, and the great holidays of celebration are just around the corner—then, if you listen carefully, you will actually hear people grow.

Chapter 3

Designing the Basic Curriculum

In designing a family-based model of catechesis, it is important that everyone in the program be on the same page. What allows such a program to work is that each family member have a common topic that they can use for discussion and interaction. As mentioned before, the standard school model for religious education arranges curriculum materials thematically around particular grade levels, e.g., grade four explores the commandments, grade five the sacraments, grade six the Bible, and so on. This type of model, therefore, is difficult to adapt to a program of intergenerational learning.

If one of your goals in making a shift in methodology is to better involve families in Sunday liturgy and renew a sense of Sabbath observance, the best solution may be to use a lectionary-based model for catechesis. In this way, you will address two needs at the same time: prayer and worship. This approach will give you a common ground to work from, so that everyone can examine the same topic on the same day. A lectionary-based curriculum also helps focus on the connections between catechesis and Sunday liturgy.

There are three lectionary readings for each Sunday in the church year. The first is usually from the Hebrew Scriptures, the second from the letters of Christian Scripture, and the third from one of the Gospels. These readings are not put together haphazardly but are selected according to the seasons of the church year. The readings for each Sunday strive for a thematic whole, with the responsorial psalm and gospel acclamation complementing this thematic whole. Usually, it is easy to see the connection between the first reading, the gospel, and the responsorial psalm. But often, it can be harder to relate the second reading to the central theme. Nonetheless, each passage from the letters was chosen to complement the other two readings, and serves a purpose within the mix. You might want to refer to a lectionary or Scripture resource to help you draw connections among all the readings. Some of these are noted in the Suggested Resources section in the back of this book.

When you are exploring the themes of a particular Sunday, be sure to read the scriptural selections carefully. Sometimes, it is only a phrase that ties them together, but each reading explores the phrase in different ways. For example, observe the following readings from the Seventeenth Sunday of the Year (Cycle B):

First reading: 2 Kings 4:42–44

A man came from Baal-shalishah bringing to Elisha, the man of God, twenty barley loaves made from the first fruits, and fresh grain in the ear. "Give it to the people to eat," Elisha said. But his servant objected, "How can I set this before a hundred men?" "Give it to the people to eat," Elisha insisted. "For thus says the Lord, 'They shall eat and there shall be some left over.'" And when they had eaten, there was some left over, as the Lord had said. The word of the Lord.

Responsorial: Psalm 145:10–11, 15–16, 17–18.

R. *The hand of the Lord feeds us; he answers all our needs.*

Let all your works give you thanks, O Lord, and let your faithful ones bless you. Let them discourse of the glory of your kingdom and speak of your might. R.

The eyes of all look hopefully to you, and you give them their food in due season; You open your hand and satisfy the desire of every living thing. R.

The Lord is just in all his ways and holy in all his works. The Lord is near to all who call upon him, to all who call upon him in truth. R.

Second reading: Ephesians 4:1–6

I plead with you as a prisoner for the Lord, to live a life worthy of the calling you have received, with perfect humility, meekness, and patience, bearing with one another lovingly. Make every effort to preserve the unity which has the Spirit as its origin and peace as its binding force. There is but one body and one Spirit, just as there is but one hope given all of you by your call. There is one Lord, one faith, one baptism; one God and Father of all, who is over all, and works through all, and is in all. The Word of the Lord.

Gospel acclamation (164): John 6:64, 69

Your words, O Lord, are spirit and life, you have the words of everlasting life.

Note: The lectionary sometime allows you to select one of several acclamations for a particular gospel; they are not as closely matched to the readings in every case.

Gospel John 6:1–15

Jesus crossed the Sea of Galilee [to the shore] of Tiberias; a vast crowd kept following him because they saw the signs he was performing for the sick. Jesus then went up the mountain and sat down there with his disciples. The Jewish feast of Passover was near; when Jesus looked up and caught sight of a vast crowds coming toward him, he said to Philip, "Where shall we buy bread for these people to eat?" (He knew well what he intended to do but he asked this to test Philip's response.) Philip replied, "Not even with two hundred days' wages could we buy loaves enough to give each of them a mouthful!"

One of Jesus' disciples, Andrew, Simon Peter's brother, remarked to him, "There is a lad here who has five barley loaves and a couple of dried fish, but what good is that for so many?" Jesus said, "Get the people to recline." Even though the men numbered about five thousand, there was plenty of grass for them to find a place on the ground. Jesus then took the loaves of bread, gave thanks, and passed them around to those reclining there; he did the same with the dried fish, as much as they wanted. When they had enough, he told his disciples, "Gather up the crusts that are left over so that nothing will go to waste." At this, they gathered twelve baskets full of pieces left over by those who had been fed by the five barley loaves.

When the people saw the sign he had performed they began to say, "This is undoubtedly the Prophet who is to come into the world." At that, Jesus realized that they would come and carry him off to make him a king, so he fled back to the mountain alone. The gospel of the Lord.

It is clear to see that *feeding* and *sustenance* are central themes of these readings. Phrases like: "The hand of the Lord feeds us," "the Lord satisfies," and "the Lord will provide" remind us that God is our provider, that God will take care of us and supply us with all we need. The faith of the apostles is also evident when they take Jesus at his word and begin to distribute the five loaves and a few dried fish. They believed Jesus would provide. The miracle underneath this story may be that such faith in Jesus led to generosity among his followers, which caused people to share their own resources.

The second reading from Ephesians directs Jesus' followers to "make every effort to preserve the unity." You will find in this reading not only a sense of comfort, but also a directive to live out the call of our baptism. After hearing these readings parishioners may walk away from the Sunday liturgy, and any subsequent catechesis, with a desire to share their resources with the needy, the hungry, and those who have yet to hear the good news. They may also be drawn to sit still sometime during the Sabbath and be fed with God's riches.

It is easy to see from this one example how one can begin to structure a program around the lectionary. This approach not only allows everyone to stay on the same page, it also gives the assembly an opportunity to really break open the readings. It encourages different ages or groups to explore different streams of the same theme. One group can center on God's providential care; another on the meaning of miracles; another on our call to feed the hungry; another on the meaning of unity in purpose; another on being fed. One central theme taken from the Sunday readings provides ample food for thought and allows entire families to be on the same page for the week.

Mapping out a calendar

The next step is to map out a calendar year, identifying the lectionary themes for each Sunday. Most parish religious education programs follow the academic year. Since summer schedules vary greatly for most parishioners, it is probably best to stay close to planning your program within the academic year.

At Corpus Christi Parish, we decided to start the program as soon as possible after Labor Day and run until Easter. In order to give people enough time to fit the religious education classes into their schedule, we sent out a registration packet to all families with school-age children at the beginning of August. (Remember, they had learned about the new structure of the program back in May.) The packet included a complete schedule of classes for the academic year.

We then asked that completed registrations be returned to the parish before the first of September. In doing so, we hoped to give religious education a high priority on the family's schedule, putting it more on par with the academic schedule and removing it a bit from other extracurricular activities, such as scouting, sports, and ballet lessons. Most teachers will tell you there is wisdom with starting right into serious course work in September and October, when students are fresh and ready to study. Once they begin to think about holidays and vacations, interest can begin to wane. So capitalize on this reality.

In mapping out your calendar, you also will have to research holidays, school vacations, and important feasts. If you are going to hold all classes on Sunday or on weekends, the best plan may be to arrange classes for every other weekend. You will find that it is extremely labor intensive when all of the religious education students *plus* their parents come together for any given session. Doing this every week would tire both planners and catechists well before the year was over. Planning a good session every other week gives people breathing room and time to really absorb what they are learning.

A general rule of thumb, then, means that there will be two sessions per month. Most of the time, this will mean that classes are held every other week, but sometimes, there may need to be classes held two weeks in a row with two weeks off in a row. If you communicate with parents early on, they are usually very understanding and appreciative of any efforts to accommodate their schedules.

As an example, here is the calendar for the religious education program at Corpus Christi for the 1999-2000 school year (see the complete outline for this year in Appendix 1). Sessions were held on the following days:

September 12 and 19

October 3, 17, and 31

November 7 and 21

December 5 and 12

January 9 and 23

February 6 and 27

March 12 and 26

April 2 and 9

Labor Day was very late in 1999, so the first Sunday after Labor Day weekend was September 12. (Other years, we have started as early as September 7.) The second weekend in October was a holiday weekend for Columbus Day. And so to avoid holding classes on this weekend, we scheduled classes for October 3 and October 17. As you can see, however, that pushed the September date back to September 19 and called for two weeks in a row in September.

While November 11 is Veterans Day and its observation may fall on a Monday, we felt it was more important to avoid having classes on Thanksgiving weekend. Also, parents usually do not mind meeting two weeks in a row in December if it means that by the second week in December, they are finished with religious education sessions until after the Christmas holidays. This does not mean that you cannot plan a Christmas pageant for the holiday season. Just emphasize that the program and rehearsals are strictly voluntary and separate from family religious education sessions. Since the first Sunday in January is still part of the Christmas season and generally children are still on vacation, religious education sessions do not resume until the weekend of the Baptism of Our Lord, a great place to pick up again. We find that after the month-long break, parents and their children are ready to come back in earnest.

In January, try to avoid scheduling classes for the Martin Luther King holiday, as families may make plans for a winter ski trip or getaway. In February, look out for Presidents Day weekend, any school vacations, and the start of Lent. There will always be parents who want to take off both the weekend before and the weekend after school vacation, but explain to folks that this is too much time away from the curriculum. Often, it is best to plan no classes for the weekend before a vacation, and hold class on the weekend after vacation, as people tend to come back more refreshed after a rest. But whatever you decide, try to stay with the schedule year after year, if possible, as this allows parents to plan ahead.

If you intend to wrap up your program by Easter, your last class may be held on Palm Sunday. Again, watch the calendar closely. If your classes will run into April, pay attention to the change for daylight savings time and to any April school vacations. In many areas of the country, spring sports programs begin as soon as daylight savings time is in effect, which can mean games and practices at all hours on weekends. The reality is that a religious education program may be in direct conflict with this schedule.

In the program at Corpus Christi, where first reconciliation and first Eucharist are both celebrated in the second grade, special celebrations for those two events are planned separate from Sunday sessions. First reconciliation is a communal celebration on a weekday evening, while first Eucharist is held on the Saturday or Sunday immediately following Easter. If you usually hold your first Eucharist in May, remember that Mothers Day falls on the second Sunday in May. This could be a possible conflict for the families in your parish.

In chapter four, we will look at other components for an intergenerational model, such as Project Sundays, where families work together as a team on a fun venture or parish outreach activity. These parts of your program should also be included in the calendar for the year. If at all possible, the entire calendar should fit on one page. This makes it easy for parents to post it on their refrigerator or in another visible location.

Do whatever you can to impress the importance of reserving the dates for religious education sessions upon the families in your parish. You might want to try some reinforcement techniques; for example, you can create bookmarks listing the dates for the sessions, and leave them at the church doors for people to pick up. Families need to know that these dates are sacrosanct.

A word on logistics and numbers

When you are talking about bringing together your entire religious education student body and at least one parent from each family (though often both will come), you are probably talking about big numbers! What space is available to accommodate the logistics of your group? The size of the program and the availability of space may necessitate some adjustments in your program. If you have ten classrooms available and an open area where seventy-five or so parents can meet, this means your program can work well for 150 children. In parishes with approximately 300 children in the program, double sessions can be held before and after one particular Mass or after two separate Masses. Perhaps you have a large parish center or school and can accommodate more than ten classes at a time. This will allow you to work with more people in the program at the same time.

Generally, religious education classes are most effective when there are ten to fifteen children in a classroom. If there are fifteen students and they are young, an additional classroom aide may be needed. You may want to add a preschool class (three and four year olds) as well as a kindergarten class, if the parish does not have them already. Larger parish centers have the option of filling all their classrooms at once, as long as there is an open separate space for the parents. Space availability in such a center is usually the deciding factor for whether a parish can hold one session or two.

You might want to try Saturday sessions either before or after the Saturday evening liturgy. If your aim is to link catechesis to liturgy and renew a sense of Sabbath, however, this time frame may not work as well. Linking catechesis to liturgy and to Sabbath is most effective when it can dovetail the Sunday liturgy in some dimension. Another alternative might be to have sessions both on Saturday evening and on Sunday morning. Split the families into two groups, and have one group come on Sunday while the other comes on Saturday.

You might also want to take a gradual approach to incorporating a family catechesis program. For the first year, have half of the families participate in the family-based intergenerational model, while the other half stays with the traditional approach. Then switch the families for the following year. This gradually gives everyone a taste of intergenerational learning, and can acquaint the entire parish with Sabbath catechesis.

Finding the lectionary readings
Once you have mapped out your calendar for the school year, it is time to identify the readings for each of the Sundays or weekends on which a session will be held. There are several ways to do this. Several Catholic publishers produce desk calendars with the lectionary readings noted for each day (for example, Paulist Press and Liturgy Training Publications). You can also find the readings in the Ordo (*The Order of Prayer in the Liturgy of the Hours and Celebration of the Eucharist*) usually published according to dioceses and sometimes kept in the sacristy or rectory. You can find the readings in a lectionary, once you know which day

of the church year falls on each Sunday that you plan to use, and which cycle (A, B, or C) you are currently in. Lectors' workbooks can also assist you. Oftentimes, parish calendars will denote which Sunday in the church's calendar falls on a particular date; for example, Sunday, September 10, 2000 was the Twenty-Third Sunday in Ordinary Time.

You should know that the church year begins on the First Sunday of Advent, which usually falls around the first Sunday of December, and that the cycle of readings changes with the First Sunday of Advent. Thus, in planning for the academic year, you will have to look at two different cycles. To see how this works, let's take the school year 2001-2002, beginning with September 9th, the Twenty-Third Sunday in Ordinary Time. From September 9th to November 25th, the readings are from Cycle C. On December 2, 2001, the readings change to Cycle A and remain in that cycle until December 1, 2002, when they move to the Cycle B readings.

The cycles move from A to B to C and then back to A again. If you are using an actual lectionary, you will find that Sundays are grouped by their name first and cycles second, so look for the readings for a particular date, then look for the liturgical title of that day (e.g., the First Sunday of Advent) and then for the cycle of the year. Now you can begin to list all the readings for each Sunday of the year.

Identifying themes and cross-referencing to the *Catechism*
The next step is to identify the theme of the readings for the day. One way to do this is to look for the teachings of the Church that are present in these readings by cross-referencing each of them to the *Catechism of the Catholic Church*. In the back of the *Catechism*, there are several indices, one of which is an index of scriptural citations. You can use this reference to see what doctrinal issues are raised by specific scriptural passages, and then

go back to find that passage within the lectionary cycle. For instance, if you were to cross index the readings from the Seventeenth Sunday in Ordinary Time, Cycle B, you would find that both 2 Kings 4:42–44 and Psalm 145 have no explicit citations. One would also find, though, that the second reading from Ephesians (4:1–6) has several: 172, 249, 814, 866, 1454, 1971, 2219 and 2790 (the *Catechism* is organized by paragraphs, from 1 to 2865; the asterisk after the paragraph number indicates that the citation has been paraphrased). The gospel for that day, John 6:1–15, also has corresponding citations to the *Catechism*: 439, 549, 559 and 1338. If you take the time to read these paragraphs, it is often far easier to determine the overall theme of the readings. For instance, if you read paragraph 549 in the *Catechism* and cross-reference it to Jesus' feeding the thousands with a few barley loaves and dried fish, a deeper meaning surfaces:

> By freeing some individuals from earthly evils of hunger, injustice, illness and death, Jesus performed messianic signs. Nevertheless he did not come to abolish all evils here below, but to free men from the greatest slavery, sin, which thwarts them in their vocation as God's sons and causes all forms of human bondage.

Using this information, you might decide that the overall theme for the Seventeenth Sunday in Ordinary Time will be: "Food : What kind do we need and how do we use it?" Each person in the family can approach this topic from a number of vantage points and at the end of the day, still have a Christian, Sabbath-centered topic of conversation for the week. So we see how the *Catechism* can help expand the theme of the readings for that day, and assist parishioners in making a connection between liturgy, catechesis, and their daily lives.

It is wise to cross-reference all the lectionary readings for the particular Sundays with the *Catechism,* as often a more subtle meaning can surface that might have an influence on the selection of an overall theme for the day. You can identify the overall theme for each Sunday in a phrase or two and communicate it to the families. A good idea is to print up the lectionary readings and the theme for each religious education session as part of your calendar and send it along to families with the registration packet. This is a positive way of inviting families to anticipate and participate in intergenerational learning.

Selecting materials

There are a number of texts and materials available that are based on the lectionary. Keep in mind your primary and secondary goals when selecting materials. If intergenerational catechesis is one goal and Sabbath connection is another, search for materials that allow you to address the specific topic through a variety of age-related venues. Remember, there are many different learning levels and styles in a mixed-age group. Balance is the key.

Take apart a given theme and divide it into sections for discussion according to age level or interest or learning style. Some materials already do this, to an extent. Most are not formatted for family groups, however, and assume that those being catechized are under sixteen or so years old. Some RCIA materials are helpful in this area, for these are always geared toward adult learning. Some adult confirmation programs address adult learning styles as well. All in all, it takes some work to find materials that can match your program. (In the Suggested Resources section of this book, you will find the names of a number of publishers with lectionary-based materials.)

Often, the most compelling way to entice parents to participate in a program is to invite speakers who have some expertise on a given theme. For instance, if your lesson focuses on the theme of hunger, perhaps a speaker from Bread for the World could be invited to discuss ways that those of us who have enough food on our tables can share with those who do not. Or, you could invite a speaker to address the topic of addiction, whether to food, to smoking, to alcohol, or even to exercise and fitness. The talk can address how a Christian can look at addiction and overcome an addiction in order to bond oneself to Christ rather than to things. There are an endless variety of options to choose from when we begin to unpack the word of God.

When you have examined all the various dimensions of a topic, it is important to make sure these dimensions tie together in some way to promote conversation among families. DREs have done their job well if families extend the catechesis beyond the celebration of liturgy and the two-hour Sunday session to the rest of the week.

Beyond the basic curriculum, there are other components that will increase the effectiveness of family-based catechesis. Let's look at a few of these now.

Chapter 4

Other Components

Early on in our religious education program, we decided to keep people interested by using a diversity of approaches as well as different topics. We encouraged our speakers to interact with parents in a variety of ways, knowing that even the best catechists need a variety of techniques to keep their presentation of the material fresh. Since this program is a family endeavor that seeks to mix generations, that dynamic is featured in Project Sundays, in the opening pancake breakfast, and in the social outreach activities. In any lectionary-based program, often some type of explicit doctrinal material needs to be included, as well.

After two years of using our new program, the religious education advisory board, as well as the DRE and some of the catechists, began to notice a gap in the overall scope of the program. Students were not necessarily learning their prayers or becoming as familiar with Catholic teaching as everyone would have liked. Even though the lectionary lessons had been cross-referenced to the *Catechism of the Catholic Church*, families were only coming together for fourteen or fifteen Sundays out of the year, and we could only cover a limited amount of material in that time. Something was still needed to teach students certain basics of the Catholic faith.

After examining a number of alternatives, two choices were made. First, we decided that each month, a particular "prayer of the month" would be assigned to all students, to learn or review. The religious education classes normally began and ended with prayer, so the monthly prayer could easily be incorporated into the classroom routine. We also decided to remind the parents of the prayer so that they could say it at home with their children during the month. Second, we decided to add the *Catechism Workbook* (published by Resources for Christian Living) to the religious education program. This series includes an edition of the workbook for grades 1 through 8, as well as an ungraded edition for use with high school students and adults (identical to the workbook for grade 8, though not labeled as such).

And so, during the third year of using an intergenerational model, the catechists began to set aside ten minutes of each class and use the *Catechism Workbook* to introduce or review basic Catholic concepts. These simple books introduce one concept per lesson and are written in a practical, definition-style format. The topics covered include: the Trinity is Father, Son, and Spirit; Jesus as both human and divine; the concept and definition of revelation; the marks of the Church; the seven sacraments; the communion of saints; devotion to Mary; sacramental signs and symbols; and the gifts of the Spirit. The workbooks were sent home between family sessions. Parents were asked to review the lesson with their children, and sometime, to look ahead to the next lesson. (Doing an entire lesson takes about ten minutes.) While it was a bit confusing the first year since different grades had a different number of lessons, a brief schedule for catechists and parents solved most scheduling concerns. Reminiscent of an older practice of "hearing one's child's Catechism," this practice was another way to extend catechesis into the home, to teach a Catholic vocabulary, and to encourage parents and children to talk with each other about their faith.

Another key component in a family model of catechesis is the social teaching of the Catholic church. Charity and justice are the two arms of the church's social teaching; they are intimately connected to the gospel and should have a central place in any lectionary-based catechetical program. In their 1971 statement, the Roman Synod of Bishops concurred that "action on behalf of justice fully appears to us as a constitutive dimension to the gospel of Jesus Christ." Since Vatican II, many Catholics have become aware of the social teachings of the Church. They realize that Jesus came not only to comfort the afflicted, but to afflict those who are too comfortable. All of us have obligations toward our brothers and sisters in the human family. Most Catholic parishes today offer all types of social outreach both within the parish and to the larger community. Many of these parishes also have active social justice committees, which sometimes tackle the harder issue of choosing justice over charity.

Try not to overlook the importance of Catholic social teaching in total catechesis. There should be something within each year's program that draws families into outreach efforts, whether as part of the religious education body or as individual families within the larger parish family. These efforts can be incorporated into some of the Project Sundays or they can stand alone, even apart from a Sunday time frame, such as seasonal activities.

You may want to consider a dramatic presentation, one that meshes entertainment with catechesis. At Corpus Christi, two such productions were used in different years: "Three and a Half Stories of Christmas" and "The Gospel of Mark." Both of these were interactive and audience friendly, and the participants were quite surprised by what they learned from this manner of catechesis. Another speaker focused his presentation on the Magnificat, which was one of the readings for that particular day. In his talk, he included some of the musical settings of this prayer and thus introduced participants to some of the rich music traditions of the church.

Elements such as drama and music provide additional ways of teaching the faith. As much as possible, these multiple mediums should be programmed into the yearly calendar well in advance.

Family Project Sundays

Since we are talking about a family program that seeks to mix generations, it is wise to have some activities during the year that bring all of the generations together at one time. In our parish, this happens at least twice a year, on what we call "Project Sundays." During these sessions, participants work as a family unit on a particular lectionary theme. The project will often involve some type of arts and crafts activity, something that Moms and Dads can work on together with their five year old, their seven year old, and their twelve year old. Many times, the resulting project becomes something that can be taken home to further extend the lesson.

One of the aims of the family projects is to get family members talking and working together on a simple project that is somehow tied to the liturgical year. Some of the projects that were tried at Corpus Christi were: making Advent wreaths for the homes; constructing a family crest on a square yard of felt that would later be used in the Palm Sunday procession; organizing and running the annual city-wide hunger walk; making miniature labyrinths that corresponded to a larger labyrinth used in the sanctuary of the church one Lent; and "pumpkin mania," where each family brought a Halloween pumpkin to church to be blessed and decorated after Mass, then delivered by individual families to parish shut-ins.

One activity for Project Sunday began as an activity for students in grades one through eight during Lent one year, but it captivated the entire parish and is now repeated yearly. Early in Lent, the children each receive a tiny, live caterpillar. They place them in small cups with some food, and then put them in a 5' x 5' x 6' netted butterfly house in the gathering area of the church. Cocoons are spun and, the Spirit willing (and, with teachers timing this as closely as possible with the supplying company), hundreds of butterflies emerge during the Triduum. It is amazing what excitement this creates for everyone in the parish, and the rich symbolism this adds to the whole resurrection experience.

You can find more details on some of the ideas for Project Sundays, mentioned above, in Appendix 4.

Parish and community outreach activities

There are a number of ways that the religious education program can reach out to the parish community or to the local community. So many outreach projects are born of the gospel messages. At Corpus Christi, the Newton Hunger Walk and the Project Sunday celebration of "Pumpkin mania" are but two examples. Many parishes have giving trees around Christmas, or gifts of love at Valentine's Day, or opportunities to assist local food pantries or homeless shelters. Some suburban parishes twin with inner city parishes.

What you do want to emphasize in these types of activities are the explicit links between the gospel and the proposed activity. For instance, if the gospel of the day is talking about water and its various powers and attributes (e.g., John 4:5–42), an outreach project built around the issue of water conservation and ecology can make the teachings of the gospel come alive for families and children. An Advent reading that emphasizes patience and waiting (e.g., Matthew 3:1–12) can be linked to a project that deals with local parenting programs, such as the Young Single Father's Program or Parents of Terminally Ill Children. Our families can reach out to other families. The gospels are full of symbols that can be translated into directives for outreach. You just need to reflect deeply on the Scriptures to identify such insights.

One project that was initiated by the parish religious education office and which eventually spilled over into the parish at large was the butterfly project mentioned before. While it was designed for the younger children, it was set up in the gathering area, so that everyone passed by it on their way into and out of church. It became a topic of conversation not only in the parish, but throughout the town. Folks from other parishes started coming to see the "butterfly house." What started as a simple project in the parish grew into an event that was embraced by the larger community. The beauty of the butterflies offered a visible sign of Christian concepts, such as dying and rising and new life. Symbols such as these cross generations and even specific religions.

Using drama, music, and art

Many people learn through sound, so this group can really benefit from using music or drama in catechesis. If people are having fun while they learn, they are naturally more engaged in the learning process. In the dramatic presentations at Corpus Christi, the audience was invited to participate. To see your neighbors acting with minimum preparation makes the event more entertaining. And remember, too, that laughter is often an excellent medium for allowing us to get the message.

Music also touches the soul. It unleashes poetry and allows space for reflection. Even Plato called for its inclusion in the building of his ideal city, and he described its influence as powerful:

> Therefore, when a man gives music an opportunity to
> charm his soul with the flute, and to pour through his ears
> as through a funnel those sweet, soft, and plaintive tunes
> we have mentioned, when he spends his whole life humming them and delighting in them, then at first, if he has
> any spirit, it is softened as iron is tempered and, from
> being hard and useless, is made useful. (*Plato's Republic*)

Employing music in catechesis, either with hymns or other types of music, can charm the soul and open one's spirit to listen and to learn. Weaving meaningful music throughout a catechetical program can only enrich the program and open the doors to learning for a variety of people. Catechists can also use music as they gather their groups together, or as a background for prayer.

Another presenter to the parish, a youth minister gifted with the ability to paint, offered a program called "Prayers to Painting" in which he told the story of Jesus' life as he continually added brush strokes to an empty canvas. By the end of the session, he had completed a life-size picture of the resurrected Christ. Everyone who witnessed this process, but especially those who are moved visually, are captivated by the use of such a medium for catechesis.

Mixing groups

Another way of changing the norm is to actually mix the students, both children and adult groups. If parents always sit at the same table week after week, they may have chosen those tables deliberately and may have become comfortable with a particular group. This needs to be respected, but it doesn't mean that tables can't be mixed now and then. Occasionally, it is good for people to hear other voices.

At times, mixing different specific groups can be a valuable asset in intergenerational catechesis. Junior high or high school students may benefit from listening to some of the speakers addressing parents. Some parents have even requested that their older children join them on occasion. This can provide an additional framework for communication between parents and adolescents. For example, if the topic for the day is "Render unto Caesar what is Caesar's," and the discussion is to focus on the separation of church and state, with practical applications of that theme—e.g., whether school prayer should be allowed or the Ten Commandments posted within the schools—young adults often have just as much to contribute to this dialogue as do their parents. Providing opportunities for such collaborative discussion is invaluable. As you map out the calendar year, the topics that might lend themselves to intergenerational discussion often will stand out.

A great way to demonstrate the connectedness of the sacraments of initiation is to invite those who are preparing for baptism or first Eucharist or confirmation to come together for a catechetical session. This can mean mixing second grade students with those in ninth or tenth grade. If the number of students in the classes is similar, you can match the students one-on-one. They can continue this relationship through the year, whether as prayer partners, through correspondence, or in a classroom setting. You might also invite catechumens to visit with younger students. This can have a remarkable effect on everyone. When young people, especially teenagers, see adults studying the faith because they want to become part of the Christian family of God, they really pay attention. By this type of ongoing interaction, the various groups in your catechetical program can learn from one another as well as build the community of a given parish and, in turn, the kingdom of God.

Another approach that works is to find opportunities to mix catechists with parents or catechists with the families. When Project Sundays are held, catechists usually have a rather informal role and may take care of passing out refreshments or helping families with an arts and crafts project. But the underlying aim here is to invite catechists to engage with their students within the family context, as well as to initiate and build relationships between the parents and the catechists. These types of encounters are invaluable. They introduce catechists to the actual family dynamic of their students and provide a mechanism for communication. The communication can occur right then and there or be extended to classroom sessions or phone calls to parents, if necessary. This interaction also provides another way for members of the community to get to know one another.

Another great way to involve parents, kids, and catechists in working together is to begin the year with a pancake breakfast. You can schedule this to begin immediately after liturgy (perhaps having the catechists serve the children and their parents!). This type of gathering gives families and catechists the chance to informally introduce themselves to each other, and sets a positive tone for the year. It also invites further collaboration in learning.

First reconciliation and first communion

In the majority of parish religious education programs young children in the second grade are being prepared for two sacraments: first reconciliation and first communion. This in itself provides a full agenda for seven year olds.

Incorporating sacrament-specific curriculum materials into a lectionary-based program can be done, but it takes a bit more planning. You will need to allocate at least twelve hour-long lessons that are sacrament specific for these children. They can still attend the same Sundays, worship together at Mass, and participate in Project Sundays. A few programs introduce the sacraments in six sessions apiece (*Together in Jesus*, available from Peter Li, Inc., is one of them). If you subtract the two Project Sundays, that sometimes allows an introductory session in which the second graders are streamlined with the rest of the lectionary-based curriculum for the first week, and then immediately switch over to first penance preparation in the fall, and first Eucharist preparation in the spring. Another alternative is to do part or all of the sacramental programs at home and include two or three parent sessions for those. Many parents understand that if they have a second grader it will be a special year and more work may be necessary.

During the course of that year, parents will continue to review the two very special events that are coming in their lives. Seeing parents every two weeks usually eliminates the need for additional meetings—unless they are doing the whole program at home. Extra time with the second graders can occur during a mini-retreat day when the children can participate in activities such as baking the bread they will later use, learning how wine is made, learning a class song, making individual banners to hang on the pews on first communion day, and touring the church with their Mom or Dad.

Chapter 5

Ongoing Evaluation

To determine the effectiveness of any program, it is necessary to put some type of evaluation mechanism in place. You will want to ask questions such as these: are the children learning what you want them to learn? Is the intergenerational approach working? Have families indeed recovered a sense of observing the Sabbath?

There are various ways to evaluate your program, and it is important to remember that everyone involved in the catechetical process should be afforded the opportunity to comment on its effectiveness. That includes not only testing the students, but asking the students as well as the parents for their opinions, approaching the catechists as to how effective they think the year has been, consulting with the religious education advisory board (which should be doing an ongoing evaluation throughout the year), and soliciting the parish staff and the pastoral council for their input. Additionally, the pastor and the other presiders will be able to tell you if more and more families are attending Sunday liturgy.

When all the voices have been heard you can begin to determine what has worked, what has not, and what needs to be changed. While there are many different ways to design tools for evaluation, here follows a sampling of a few:

1. Student testing

If one of the reasons for changing the program in the first place was a concern that the children were not learning what they should, a simple test can be administered either once or twice during the year. In the aftermath of Vatican II, there was a concerted effort in religious education to have students understand the curriculum, rather than just memorize it. This attitude engendered some resistance to testing. If you want to determine what students understand as well as what they have absorbed, however, there are ways to do that. There are no cries of protest in English classes when students are tested on the meaning of works by Shakespeare or Longfellow, or in history classes when students are tested on events and specific occurrences. It can be done.

At Corpus Christi, we decided to test near the end of the spring semester. If you have expanded your program to include a preschool class and a kindergarten class, you will be testing children from age three or four through the teenage years. Some people advocate not testing the younger grades and beginning with first grade. That is certainly an option, but whatever you decide, keep in mind the appropriateness of the test for the age level of the students. For children who cannot yet read or write, oral games can be played to determine what has been learned. Drawing or verbal communication can be other options, and games that demonstrate actual learning can be incorporated into the testing. It is usually best to give catechists a wide berth in designing those tests. They are the ones who have been working with the students during the year, they know what they have covered, and they usually know their students fairly well.

Another question that may arise is this: how can you put together a test covering three or four months worth of material and expect the children to do well when they only meet every other week? If the catechists are told at the beginning of the year that there will be one or two tests and given approximate times for these tests, they can plan their lessons accordingly. They know the important points they want to cover during the year. Each class can include time to review material, and there are a variety of ways to do this. In a lectionary-based program that also involves Mass attendance, it is sometimes helpful to give the children a small snack, just to break up the two-hour time frame. A catechist may want to do a short review each session while the children are eating their snacks. You can also include memory games or hang class posters with important points to learn during the year.

It is important to allow the catechists to design the tests as well as any study devices they will use during class time or to take home to help students prepare for the test. After the testing is done, catechists can then correct the tests and give them to the DRE, who can evaluate them further and give them to the parents. Parents then have the opportunity to discuss with their children how they did on the tests.

When we first introduced testing, there was a little opposition from parents, but not much. Students were extremely nervous the first time around. When everyone began to see, however, that the purpose of the testing was not to fail anyone but to create a more effective program, it rapidly gained support. At first, very few of the parents seemed interested in knowing the test results. But gradually more began to want to see if their child was also doing well in the religious education program. Every year, we find that more and more parents interact with their children by talking about the test results.

2. Parent evaluations

An equally important dimension in program evaluation is to get the reaction and evaluation of parents. While some parents may have been involved in planning the new religious education model, it is imperative that all parents involved in the program be given a forum for evaluation. Again, this can be done once or twice a year. If you want a critique of speakers, it is helpful to do an evaluation at least twice a year, or even after each session. To try to remember in April what a speaker said or did the previous October is somewhat difficult. You can design a form that will allow parents to write down their reflections regarding each speaker or each session. If you are only going to have parents evaluate the speakers once or twice a year, it may be helpful to offer a brief description of what occurred in a particular session. If, for instance, one of the sessions involved drama or mixed junior high students with parents, include that information in the description.

Another technique that works well is to combine the parent evaluations with a written or verbal report on the overall test scores of the children. This way, parents can judge the effectiveness of the program with regard to what the children are learning. No names need to be provided on the information, but classes can be listed with a brief description of the type of test, such as oral, game format, multiple choice, essay, or combination, including both individual grades and a class average. For example, a sixth grade test could be described as one that consisted of true and false, multiple choice, and fill in the blanks, with individual scores of 64, 69, 75, 77, 79, 81, 84, 84, 87, 88, 90 and 91, and a class average of 80.75. This way, the parents have a general idea of how the students in particular grades did during the year. If possible, they should also be provided with all class scores so they can view the results of the entire student body. This is helpful when, for example, a particular class does poorly and the DRE suggests remedial summer review work. (Usually it only takes one year of low scores and subsequent extra work during the summer before students begin to pay more attention to classes and tests.)

If parent evaluations are only done once a year, at the closing session, there must be some means of communication to report back to the parents as well as to the religious education advisory board, the parish pastoral council, and the pastoral staff what the parents have said. This information can be gathered in the form of a report that is distributed to the parents and to the other groups in the parish before the summer begins. In this way, if parents have suggestions for items such as more mixed groups, more Project Sundays, more concentration on students learning prayers, or more participation in liturgy, some of these suggestions can be incorporated into the overall program during summer planning.

If changes are being made because of parent suggestions, an explanation should accompany these changes when they are included in next year's program. Of course, any suggestions made by parents have to be carefully weighed before any change in a program is made. Have you considered the numbers? In other words, if two parents want to extend the year through June but the majority of parents do not, then although you must listen carefully and consider both viewpoints, it is clear in which direction to move. Likewise, if a good number of parents appreciate the arts and crafts dimension of Project Sundays and want to see this replace many of the ordinary classes, but the DRE and catechists know that they cannot teach all that they need to teach with more arts and crafts activities, then this reality will need to be explained to the parents.

Ultimately, you have to base any changes and decisions made on your initial educational objectives as well as on the numbers. Also, theological and educational expertise have to be considered when making changes. But the more communication that can be realized between the parents and the parish, the more successful any program will be. Parents want their children catechized. Usually, by the end of the first year, they also recognize that this means they must continue to learn with their children and that lifelong catechesis is indeed a parish-wide effort.

3. Catechist evaluations

Another major evaluation has to come from the catechists them-selves. They are often the ones best able to judge whether the children are learning and whether they have successfully accom-plished what they set out to do.

There are a variety of ways for catechists to evaluate the pro-gram, but often the most effective is at teacher meetings. The number of catechists in your program may dictate how many meetings you set aside for evaluation. It is often easier to group catechists around the age groups they teach, for instance, pre-school through first grade or preschool through fourth grade, then grades five through eight, grades nine through twelve, and so on. The DRE can set aside a group of end-of-the-year evalua-tion meetings, or there may be a series of them held during the year. If you already have regularly scheduled teacher meetings during the year, evaluation should be an ongoing part of those meetings.

It will be up to the DRE to gather the input of the catechists at the end of the year and include their perceptions in the overall evaluation of the program. A listing of the sessions held during the year with their matching lectionary theme can help refresh the catechist's memories of how well their class learned during a specific week. The use of the prayer of the month technique, the *Catechism Workbook*, the lectionary materials, Project Sundays, outreach efforts—all of these components need to be individu-ally evaluated by the teachers. Parent communication and any discipline problems should also be evaluated. You will find, though, that in a family-centered program, discipline problems almost disappear. If Mom or Dad are already on the premises, Johnny or Gabriella are not going to misbehave as readily as they may have before. Since at least one parent is present at each session, communication problems between the catechist and parents also dwindle.

While listening is a key part of the evaluation process, it is helpful to write down as much material as possible, especially if there are a lot of catechists. A finalized catechist report should be drafted from all the ideas and summaries of the catechists.

4. The religious education advisory board

As mentioned earlier, the value of a religious education advisory board or commission can be inestimable. They walk with the DRE throughout the entire year's program, and should provide ongoing insights and critiques. It will be their task to help the DRE gather all the information from student tests, parent reports, and catechist evaluations and then to judge whether or not the program has been successful. Along with the DRE, the board answers the question: have the goals and directives set in the beginning of the process been realized? Why or why not?

After all the evaluations have been gathered, it is up to the board to articulate once more their goals in launching a catechetical process for the entire parish. They will have to look at the issue of Mass attendance and participation: has it significantly increased? If yes, what was done to effect this increase? If no, what can be tried to encourage better attendance at Sunday liturgy? Another area for the board to consider is whether the parents are more involved in their children's catechesis than they were a year before. Are the parents learning as well? Is the religious education community intersecting with the wider parish community? If yes, good. If no, what can be done to ensure that this begins to happen? If the parish has a mission statement, is the catechetical program furthering that mission statement? Is the good news of Jesus Christ becoming more widely known and understood because of the efforts of the program?

These and a vast array of other questions should occupy the thoughts of the religious education board. It is their task to judge the triumphs, the failures, and the accomplishments of the religious education program over the course of the year. The board's evaluation is the final piece of material that the DRE must use in presenting his or her report to the parish.

Budget and cost analysis

One other component that is helpful to provide is some type of picture about the overall cost of this program. If a budget report of monies coming into the religious education program as well as expenses for the program are included in the DRE's final report, this will assist the pastor and the parish council in their overall task of evaluation. During the year, the DRE should keep a list of all expenses, including texts, class materials, and speakers' fees. These will have to be weighed against any fees charged to families for the religious education program. Many parishes are now computer literate and can easily access this information from the parish's budget reports.

You will find that costs vary with a family model of catechesis. Since most lectionary-based programs generally use textual material that is either in magazine format or on duplicating sheets, there are usually no actual textbooks involved. Lectionary materials are certainly not free, but the cost of purchasing them, as well as paying stipends for speakers or other presenters, can be less than or close to the same cost as purchasing student textbooks and teacher editions. The cost of the *Catechism Workbooks* is minimal, especially in relation to a graded text. Project Sundays can cost quite a bit, depending on the type of project chosen. Parents readily understand this, however. If they see quality materials being used for a quality product that is going back to their home, they are usually willing to pay more for supplies. Putting out a basket for donations on Project Sundays is a good way to help defray the costs of these materials.

The final report

When the DRE finalizes his or her report, it should include the students' test scores, the parents' report, the catechists' report, and religious education board's report as well as a budget and cost analysis of the program. And don't forget the DRE's personal reflections on the overall program.

This report is then presented to the pastor, the parish staff, and to the parish council. Ultimately, it is the pastor's responsibility to ensure that the religious education program in his parish is healthy, but in most parishes, the parish staff and the pastoral council are part of that process, as well. A good report can give the pastor confidence in his catechetical staff. It can also be a great asset when the bishop wants to know the status of the religious education program in the parish!

Conclusion

A family-based catechetical program such as "Retrieving the Sabbath" can be a great success for any parish that wants to mesh Sabbath observances with catechesis. It proposes a different path to travel rather than the conventional religious education curriculum of the past, but it is an exciting road which affords community building alongside catechesis.

A program such as this recalls the practices of first-century Christians. It gathers believers around the table of the Lord, and reminds parents of today to slow down, savor the goodness of creation, and pause to see God's reflection in their children's eyes. It can assist all of us to learn more about ourselves and about our God, and to help us "make disciples of all nations, baptizing them in the name of the Father and of the Son and of the Holy Spirit....And remember, I am with you always to the end of the age" (Mt 28:19–20).

Sample Curricula for One Year

Here is a sample year of lectionary readings with references to the *Catechism of the Catholic Church*. This schedule was prepared for the school year 1999-2000, starting in Cycle A and moving to Cycle B.

September 12—Twenty-fourth Sunday in Ordinary Time
Opening liturgy for religious education program
   • Theme: How can the virtue of mercy touch our lives?
First reading: Sirach 27:30—28:7
   Catechism citations: none
Second reading: Romans 14:7–9
   Catechism citations: 668, 953
Third reading: Matthew 18:21–35
   Catechism citations: 982, 2227, 2843, 2845

September 19—Twenty-fifth Sunday in Ordinary Time
Special event: Pancake breakfast, with catechists as cooks and servers
   • Theme: We are laborers in God's vineyard
First reading: Isaiah 55:6–9
   Catechism citations: none
Second reading: Philippians 1:20–24, 27
   Catechism citations: 1005, 1010, 1011, 1021, 1025, 1692, 1698
Third reading: Matthew 20:1–16
   Catechism citations: none

October 3—Twenty-seventh Sunday in Ordinary Time
Preschool class has a special role in liturgy
  • Theme: What are the issues of homelessness today?
First reading: Isaiah 5:1–7
  Catechism citations: 755
Second reading: Philippians 4:6–9
  Catechism citations: 1803, 2633
Third reading: Matthew 21:33–43
  Catechism citations: 443, 755, 756

October 17—Twenty-ninth Sunday in Ordinary Time
Kindergarten class has a special role in liturgy
  • Theme: Christian stewardship and civic responsibilities.
First reading: Isaiah 45:1, 4–6
  Catechism citations: 304
Second reading: 1 Thessalonians 1:1–5
  Catechism citations: none
Third reading: Matthew 22:15–21
  Catechism citations: 2242

October 31—Thirty-first Sunday in Ordinary Time
Project Sunday: Pumpkin mania (for the shut-ins)
  • Theme: Those who humble themselves shall be exalted
First reading: Malachi 1:14—2:2, 8–10
  Catechism citations: 238, 1540
Second reading:1 Thessalonians 2:7–9, 13
  Catechism citations: none
Third reading: Matthew 23:1–12
  Catechism citations: 526, 2367

November 7—Thirty-second Sunday in Ordinary Time
First grade has a special role in liturgy
  • Theme: First-century perspectives on the end of the world
First reading: Wisdom 6:12–16
  Catechism citations: none
Second reading: 1 Thessalonians 4:13–18
  Catechism citations: 649, 989, 1001, 1012, 1025, 1687
Third reading: Matthew 25:1–13
  Catechism citations: 672, 796, 1618

November 21—Feast of Christ the King
Enrollment of the second grade at liturgy
 • Theme: Connecting the millenniums with charity
First reading: Ezekiel 34:11–12, 15–17
  Catechism citations: 754
Second reading: 1 Corinthians 15:20–26, 28
  Catechism citations: 130, 294, 411, 632, 655, 668, 671, 674, 991, 1008, 1050, 1060, 1130, 1326, 2550, 2804, 2855
Third reading: Matthew 25:31–46
  Catechism citations: 331, 544, 598, 671, 678, 679, 1033, 1034, 1038, 1373, 1397, 1503, 1825, 1932, 2443, 2447, 2449, 2463, 2831

December 5—Second Sunday in Advent
Third grade has a special role in liturgy
 • Theme: Preparing children for the wonder of Christmas
First reading: Isaiah 40:1–5, 9–11
  Catechism citations: 719, 754
Second reading: 2 Peter 3:8–14
  Catechism citations: 671, 677, 1037, 1043, 1405, 2822
Third reading: Mark 1:1–8
  Catechism citations: 422, 515

December 12—Third Sunday in Advent
Fourth grade has a special role in liturgy
 • Theme: The year of favor is upon us
First reading: Isaiah 61:1–2, 10–11
  Catechism citations: 436, 695, 714, 716, 1286
Responsorial: Magnificat: Luke 1:46–48, 49–50, 53–54
  Catechism citations: 148, 273, 706, 722, 971, 2097, 2465, 2599, 2619, 2675, 2676, 2807, 2827
Second reading: 1 Thessalonians 5:16–24
  Catechism citations: 367, 696, 1174, 2633, 2638, 2648, 2742, 2757
Third reading: John 1:6–8, 19–28
  Catechism citations: 575, 613, 717, 719

December 14
First reconciliation (7:00 PM)

Christmas Break

January 9—Baptism of Our Lord
• Theme: Baptism and our call to holiness
First reading: Isaiah 42:1–4, 6–7
  Catechism citations: 536, 555, 580, 713
Second reading: Acts 10:34–38
  Catechism citations: 438, 453, 486, 761, 1289
Third reading: Mark 1:7–11
  Catechism citations: 151, 422

January 23—Third Sunday in Ordinary Time
Fifth grade has a special role in liturgy
• Theme: Perspectives on repentance, call, and conversion
First reading: Jonah 3:1–5, 10
  Catechism citations: none
Second reading: 1 Corinthians 7:29–31
  Catechism citations: 1619
Third reading: Mark 1:14–20
  Catechism citations: 541, 787, 1423, 1427

February 6—Fifth Sunday in Ordinary Time
Sixth grade has a special role in liturgy
• Theme: How do we bless one another?
First reading: Job 7:1–4, 6–7
  Catechism citations: 441
Second reading: 1 Corinthians 9:16–19, 22–23
  Catechism citations: 24, 876
Third reading: Mark 1:29–39
  Catechism citations: 2602

February 27—Eighth Sunday in Ordinary Time
Seventh grade has a special role in liturgy
• Theme: New directions in parish ministry: home health programs
First reading: Hosea 2:16b, 17b, 21–22
  Catechism citations: 441
Second reading: 2 Corinthians 3:1b–6
  Catechism citations: 700, 859

Third reading: Mark 2:18–22
  Catechism citations: 796

March 5—Sacrament of Confirmation

March 12—First Sunday in Lent
Project Sunday: "The Gospel of Mark," a two-act play (with pizza!)
  • Theme: The "covenant of the rainbow"; renewal of covenants
First reading: Genesis 9:8–15
  Catechism citations: 56, 2569
Second reading: 1 Peter 3:18–22
  Catechism citations: 128, 632, 845, 1094, 1219, 1794
Third reading: Mark 1:12–15
  Catechism citations: 333, 538, 541, 1423, 1427

March 26—Third Sunday in Lent
Eighth and ninth grade have a special role in liturgy
  • Theme: Separation of church and state
First reading: Exodus 20:1–17
  Catechism citations: 1456, 2056, 2061, 2083, 2141, 2167, 2169,
  2196, 2200, 2214, 2257, 2330, 2400, 2463, 2504, 2513, 2533
Second reading: 1 Corinthians 1:22–25
  Catechism citations: 272
Third reading: John 2:13–25
  Catechism citations: 473, 575, 583, 584, 586, 994

April 2—Fourth Sunday in Lent
  • Theme: Why did God send his only begotten Son into the world?
First reading: 2 Chronicles 36:14–16, 19–23
  Catechism citations: 2172
Second reading: Ephesians 2:4–10
  Catechism citations: 211, 654, 1003, 1073, 2796
Third reading: John 3:14–21
  Catechism citations: 219, 444, 454, 458, 678, 679, 706, 2130

April 9—Fifth Sunday in Lent
  • Theme: The meaning of Holy Week for families
First reading: Jeremiah 31:31–34
  Catechism citations: 64, 368, 580, 715, 762, 1965, 2713

Second reading: Hebrews 5:7–9
   Catechism citations: 609, 612, 617, 1009, 2606, 2741, 2825
Third reading: John 12:20–33
   Catechism citations: 363, 434, 542, 550, 607, 662, 786, 1428, 2731, 2795, 2853

April 16—Palm Sunday
Families included in the entrance procession

April 23—Easter Sunday
Alleluia! Christ is Risen!

April 29—30
Archdiocesan Pilgrimage 2000: all families invited to participate

May 6—First Eucharist

May 12—Mother's Day
May crowning with first communicants

Suggested Resources

Lectionary Materials

Living the Good News/ Morehouse Group
600 Grant Street, Suite 400
Denver, CO 80203
1-800-824-1813
e-mail = Morehouse@Morehousegroup.com
Materials for preschool, Kindergarten, primary and intermediate grades, junior high, teens, and adults.

Pflaum Gospel Weeklies
330 Progress Road
Dayton, OH 45449
1-800-543-4383, ext. 136
e-mail: Service@HiTimePflaum.com
Materials for preschool, Kindergarten, primary and intermediate grades, and junior high, with various supplements.

Seasons of Faith (Brown-Roa)
Harcourt Religion Publishers
1665 Embassy West Drive Suite 200
Dubuque, IA 5222002-2259
1-800 922-7696
e-mail: www.harcourtreligion.com
Materials for preschool, Kindergarten, primary and intermediate grades, junior high, senior high, adults, and home resource supplements.

Albertus, Karen. *Come and See: An RCIA Process Based on the Complete Lectionary.* Cincinnati, Ohio: St. Anthony Messenger Press, 1990.

The Faith Connection (weekly bulletin inserts built around lectionary themes). Thomas More Publishing, 200 E. Bethany Drive, Allen, TX 75002; 1-800-611-6626; rclweb.com

Gallagher, Maureen, Jean Marie Hiesberger and David Woeste. *Family Time: Liturgical Catechesis for Families.* Allen, Texas: Resources for Christian Living, 1995.

Myers, Susan. *Workbook for Lectors and Gospel Readers*, U.S. edition. Chicago: Liturgy Training Publications, 2001.

Powell, Karen Hinman and Joseph P. Sinwell, eds. *Breaking Open the Word of God: Cycles A, B, C.* New York: Paulist Press, 1986, 1987, 1988.

Catholic Teaching

Resources for Christian Living (RCL)
200 East Bethany Drive
Allen, Texas 75013
1-800 822-6701; 1-800-688-8356 (FAX)
e-mail = www.rclweb.com
Publishes Our Catholic Identity, *a simple workbook based on the* Catechism of the Catholic Church, *for grades 1-8 with an ungraded adult edition (Note: ungraded edition is identical to the eighth grade text without indicating it is eighth grade). Most lessons are two pages long and can be easily used as a class supplement or for home review.*

Loyola Press
3441 North Ashland Avenue
Chicago, IL 60657
1-800-621-1008; 1-773-281-0555
e-mail = www.loyolapress.org
Publishes Knowing Our Catholic Faith, *a graded (1 through 8) workbook series on Catholic teaching. Lessons contains puzzles and fun projects, but are lengthy. Selected ones can be used as supplement for lectionary programs and others can be used at home to reinforce concepts.*

Sample agendas, bulletin announcements, and letters

Although the model for family-based catechesis used in this book was developed at Corpus Christi Parish in Newton, Massachusetts, another parish in Massachusetts, Our Lady of Sorrows in Sharon, began implementing the program this year. The samples given here are taken from Our Lady of Sorrows.

Sample agenda for a presentation to the parish council

Topic: Intergenerational catechesis and adult formation

I. Outline philosophical shift in religious education program, using *Our Hearts Were Burning Within Us* as a guide
  • Family catechesis is one of five recommended learning models from the bishops. Others are through liturgy, small group learning, large group learning, and individual study.
  • Begin a shift in parish catechesis from a graded approach for grades one through eight, to an intergenerational model. (The graded approach would remain available for those who, for one reason or another, cannot participate in an intergenerational model.)

II. Definitions
  Intergenerational means mixing generations, including preschool children, elementary- and intermediate-age children, preteens and teens, parents and/or grandparents; other adults in the parish can be invited to participate.
  Family catechesis refers to a program which involves children from

75

preschool children through those in eighth grade, with at least one parent or grandparent attending religious education sessions together with the children.

Catechesis is a Greek word that means "echoing." The practical application of this word tells us that not only do we grow in faith by passing along information to one another, we do so by sharing our faith with one another.

Project Sundays are days on which the family works together as a family unit, along with other families, on some project. These are held twice every academic year.

III. Identify program shifts:

1. We will continue to use lectionary-based materials for grades one through six.

2. We will change to lectionary-based materials for students in grades seven and eight.

3. Families will come together twice a month from September through May.

4. Every session will include attendance at Sunday liturgy, and each grade will have an opportunity to have a special role at one or two of the Masses.

5. During most of the sessions, students will go to graded classes after Mass while their parents hear from a speaker who will address the same lectionary topic. (Option: during some of the sessions, students in grades seven and eight will be invited to join their parents for the speaker's presentation.)

6. In at least two of the sessions, project Sundays will be designed (similar to the Advent workshop) where each family works together as a team.

IV. More catechists will be needed

While the ideal is that catechists in this program be persons who don't have children in religious education (in order for the parents to participate in the program), this change may take several years to be realized. A concerted effort will be made in the spring to invite and train non-parent catechists for the following September. The pool of catechists can include married couples without children, parents of infants or parents of older students, senior parishioners, and single adults.

V. Miscellaneous

• Identify the number of students, number of classes for each grade, and the location of the classes, including parent sessions. Address how the average Sunday class will be organized.

• Refreshments will be provided after liturgy for both children and parents. This will be organized by the DRE and parents.

VII. Support

It is important that the leadership of the parish, including the parish council, supports this endeavor. Also, it is key that everyone in the parish pray for this change in catechetical direction.

Sample bulletin announcements

Announcement for Week One
We are in the process of preparing a new model of religious education for the parish that will begin in September. During the next few weeks, we will learn a little more each week about this program.

In a document written last year by the U.S. Catholic bishops, titled *Our Hearts Were Burning Within Us*, the bishops asked all parishes to provide more opportunities for adult religious education. One of the ways they recommend doing this is with a family, or intergenerational, model for religious education. And so, over the course of the next three years, we will begin to move away from a graded model of religious education (weekly classes for first grade, second grade, third grade, etc.) to a family model with bi-monthly classes for the whole family.

Families in the intergenerational model will meet on two Sundays a month for two hours. The program requires that at least one parent attend Sunday liturgy with their child(ren), then the parent session held after Mass while the children are in separate classes according to grade level. Those attending the family classes on Sunday will not have to attend any further sessions during the week.

During the first year of this program, there will be room for 135 students and their parents. Registration will be on a first come, first served basis. More information will follow next week.

Announcement for Week Two

As announced in last week's bulletin, we will be running two religious education programs next fall: one, a family program that will meet twice a month on Sunday mornings for two hours, and the regular graded program of classes that meet during the week.

The family program will always include Sunday liturgy. Why should Mass be a part of catechesis? In the *Didache*, a book written in the early days of Christianity, there are clear directions for incorporating worship at the Eucharist into the initiation and education of all Christians. Today, the *General Directory for Catechesis* (GDC), written by the bishops of the United States, tells us that liturgy is linked to catechesis in order to call people together in faith. The entire Sunday experience, then—rest and re-creation of the spirit, delighting in the Lord, nourishment through the word and Eucharist—is caught up in the work of catechesis. All of us, whether as learners or as catechists, are invited to gather around the table of the Lord to refresh and renew one another.

Announcement for Week Three

During the previous two weeks, we have learned that there will be two parallel catechetical programs offered here in the fall, one a family model and one a graded model. We also learned that the family model will be closely tied to the Sunday liturgy.

In both programs, students will be using a lectionary-based approach to catechesis. This means that the classroom lessons will be based on the Sunday readings which are heard at Mass. Students from grades three through eight will also use the *Catholic Identity Workbook*, which covers basic information about Catholicism that may not come up in the Scriptures.

The family model uses a thematic approach to religious education, which means that both parents and children will study the same theme found in the readings for a given Sunday. This way, families will have a common topic to discuss and explore further when they are finished with each Sunday session. In most cases, students will be using the same curriculum materials in the fall that they are using now, although the way in which they will be used may be different. This common curriculum should help smooth our transition from one model to the other, and should help keep all our students together.

Announcement for Week Four
During the last few weeks, we have learned that there will be two types of religious education models offered for next September: the regular graded approach and a new family model.

The regular graded classes will use the same curriculum as the family model, but these classes will meet every week on a weekday for one hour. Children in the second grade will continue to prepare for the Eucharist the same way they do now, whether they are in the family model or the graded model, using a home-based program. First penance will also use a home-based program for second graders

"Class Masses" are a wonderful way to help our children learn more about their Catholic identity, as well as teach them about the Mass. We hope to continue this practice for all students, whether they are in the family program or the graded program. This means that, once a year, each grade level will participate in a special way at a particular liturgy. We also hope to have special penance services twice a year, in Advent and Lent, for all students in grades three through eight, whether they are in the family or graded models.

Our youth ministry is a vital part of our religious formation efforts, and so we will continue to invite and involve all seventh and eighth graders in special activity nights, as well as in using the Youth Center on Friday evenings, in the teen Masses, and in community service projects. We want to keep the all good things that already work well for our youth ministry, while enhancing it with new opportunities.

Announcement for Week Five

During the last few weeks we have been learning about the upcoming opportunity for intergenerational catechesis this September. Week by week, we have learned more about how this family model of religious education will operate.

This week we will talk about Project Sundays. These are Sundays on which families will still gather for Eucharist, but following the liturgy, there will be a family project that all family members will work on together. On Project Sundays, parents and children have an opportunity to actually work together and talk with one another as they learn more about their faith. This is also a good way for the families in the religious education program to connect with each other as they work together, side-by-side.

Project Sundays will feature activities such as putting together an Advent wreath or a lenten labyrinth; making banners with a family crest that could be used in a future liturgy; or taking on larger projects, such as hosting a hunger walk for the town or planning a voter registration Sunday.

Letters will be going out this week announcing our new religious education program opportunities for September. There will be an open meeting for everyone in the parish on Thursday, April 26th at O'Connell Hall from 7:30 to 9:00 PM, where you can get more information, ask questions, or get further clarification. Registration forms will be distributed during the open meeting.

Sample letter announcing an open parish meeting

Dear Parishioners,

Recently, the United States bishops released a new pastoral letter on religious education titled *Our Hearts Were Burning Within Us*. In it, the bishops are asking all of us to redirect some of our educational energies toward adults. This is not to say that we are to do any less for our children. Indeed, we are to "pledge to support adult faith formation without weakening our commitment to our other essential educational ministries" (#6).

That being said, the bishops have also suggested five ways in which to accomplish this: 1. through the liturgy; 2. through small group study (like our Bible study or theology study groups); 3. through large group study (like our lecture series); 4. through individual study (for which we have ample supplies in the church and in the religious education center); and 5. through family or intergenerational study. It is this last area that we will address here.

Family catechesis, or intergenerational learning, is one of the best ways to introduce more opportunities for adult faith formation while devoting time to the catechesis of our children. With a family model for religious education, various generations can share faith with one another and learn from one another. And this is the heart of catechesis.

The parish staff and the religious education advisory board have spent one year developing a plan to incorporate family catechesis into our current religious education program. During the first year, we hope to offer the family model of catechesis to approximately one-third of our students in grades one through eight and their parents, as well as to any other interested adults. This will not be the only model available for religious education. We will continue to have regular graded classes that will meet during the week, and families will have the option to continue in this program.

The family program will meet twice a month on Sunday for two hours, from September to May. These meetings will include attendance at liturgy. The curriculum for both the family and the graded programs will be lectionary-based; that is, the lessons will focus on the readings from the Sunday liturgy. During most of the sessions, students will learn at their grade level about the readings of the day while parents have a chance to explore the same readings with various speakers from our area. Twice a year, we will have Project Sundays, where families will work together as a family unit. There also will be additional family outreach activities during the year.

On Thursday, April 26th, we will have an open meeting at O'Connell

Hall from 7:30-9:00 PM, to further discuss these new directions in cate-chesis and answer any of your questions. Registration for both programs will begin on May 1. There are 135 student slots open for the family pro-gram, and registration will be on a first come, first served basis.

One other thing to note: because we will be running two programs at once, and we want parents free to enjoy their own sessions, we will be looking for several new catechists. After all, it does take a whole vil-lage—parish, that is—to raise a child in the faith. And it takes a whole parish village to educate one another in the faith. To address this need, Father Bob, Deacon Mike, and DRE Karen will be offering an exciting, four-part teacher training program on four Wednesdays this spring: on May 23 and 30, and on June 6 and 13. Be assured that we will need everyone's help to redirect our catechetical energies.

Please mark your calendars for the parish meeting on April 26 at 7:30 PM. See you there!

In Christ Jesus,

[The leadership of Our Lady of Sorrows Parish]

Sample agenda for parish-wide meeting:

Opening prayer
Welcome
Brief introduction to program
History of study by religious education advisory board
Theology and catechetical imperatives behind shift in models
Role of the *Catechism of the Catholic Church*
Questions and answers
Registration information
Closing prayer

Ideas for Project Sundays

Pumpkin mania

This Project Sunday mixes social outreach with a Sabbath theme. On the Sunday closest to All Saints' Day or Thanksgiving, each family is asked to bring a pumpkin to Mass, where the pumpkins are blessed. Following the liturgy, the families gather to decorate their pumpkins with markers, fabric trims, buttons, or some good, old-fashioned carving. (When parents are working with their own children, supervising tool use becomes a non-issue.) Ahead of time, the DRE or other members of the parish staff have researched the names and addresses of shut-ins or seniors in the parish who might appreciate a decorated pumpkin for the holidays.

After the families are finished with their decorating, they each are given the name and address of the parishioner (who has already been called and is expecting a visit from a family), and asked to deliver the pumpkin that same afternoon. This is a great way to teach social outreach to children, to tie it in to the gospel message, and to build community within the parish.

Advent wreaths

Seasonal times during the church year offer great opportunities for catechesis to spill over into the home. And so each year we encourage our families to construct an Advent wreath for their own home.

You will need fresh evergreens, an oasis ring (available at florists), three purple candles and one pink candle, matching ribbons, dried pink, purple, and white flowers, and wooden florist pics with wire for attaching flowers and ribbons to the wreath. It is imperative that all supplies be set out for each family at the tables beforehand as you will only have one hour to complete this project.

A finished sample of a wreath should be available at the front of the room, and a step-by-step instruction sheet can be placed on each table. You might also want to make up an Advent prayer booklet that contains basic prayers for the families to take home and use when lighting the wreath on each of the four Sundays.

Here is a sample of a step-by-step instruction sheet:

1. While you enjoy your snack and beverage, take a few minutes to introduce yourself to the other people at your table if you don't already know them.

2. We will be making our Advent wreaths out of fresh greens, dried flowers, ribbons, and candles. To begin, cut small pieces of boxwood on an angle and insert into oasis. Always insert the boxwood in the same direction around the oasis.

3. After you have filled in the oasis ring with boxwood, attach the dried flowers to the florist's pics, then tie on a ribbon. Make a half dozen or so, and then insert the pics into the oasis, evenly spaced.

4. Add extra greens if you wish. Some cedar and holly are available, but be careful not to use too much as the scent can be overpowering.

5. Place the four candles into wreath and twist into place. (You may want to remove the candles when you leave here, and reattach them once you get home.) Generally, three purple candles and one pink are used during Advent. You can replace all the candles with four new white ones at Christmas, if you wish.

6. When you take your wreath home, mist it once a week, or submerge it in water once or twice during the season (being careful not to wet the dried flowers). With a little bit of care and attention, your wreath should last and look fresh until February.

Family crest banners

For this project, cut felt or another heavyweight fabric into pieces measuring approximately one square yard each. Then sew a two-inch casing along the top of one side. At each table, provide a pre-cut banner for each family, fabric glue, scissors, various scraps of fabric, markers, and some rick-rack or miscellaneous trims (a great way to collect these is to ask folks to clean out their sewing supply kits and donate the scraps). Also have on hand patterns for letters of the alphabet and religious symbols, cut out of heavy stock paper, which families can use in creating their banner.

Encourage the families to design their own family crest in any way they desire. They can include symbols of things that are important to them, e.g., a specific sport or their home or their pets. They may also want to include some religious symbols that emphasize their faith. When the banners have been completed, let them lay flat to dry. You can buy yardsticks in bulk and give one to each family to insert in the casing, or use one-inch thick dowels that have been cut into three-foot-long pieces.

At our parish, we make the family crest banners in the spring. When the banners are complete, we keep them at the parish. Then, on Palm Sunday, we gather the families together before Mass and give them their banner to carry in procession. What a colorful way to begin the liturgy! The families then take the banners home after Mass.

This project can also be adapted to use with your second grade families in making banners for first Eucharist.

Lenten labyrinths
The labyrinth is an ancient pattern of circles, somewhat like a maze. Unlike a maze, however, there is only one way to the center and one way out. People walk the path of a labyrinth, meditating as they go along their journey to the center and then back out again. The twists and turns symbolize life's peaks and valleys, but the path always goes one way: to God, through grace.

In our parish one year, we decided that a labyrinth would be an ideal prayer form to use during Lent. It was determined that a labyrinth could fit in the sanctuary of the church. Also, because the sanctuary in most churches is a special space, locating the labyrinth here would enhance the prayer experience. While the labyrinth was in place, parishioners were invited to stop by the church and experiment with this ancient prayer form. Many parishioners tried it and found it to be an enriching experience. At the same time, the catechists introduced the concept of prayer with the labyrinth to their students.

To make a labyrinth prayer wheel, find a picture of a labyrinth, whether in a book about this prayer form, or in a book about the great cathedrals of the Middle Ages, particularly Chartres. Make copies of the labyrinth, enough for all the families, to fit on a square block of wood, 3/4" thick and approximately twelve to eighteen inches long on each side. On Project Sunday, provide markers and crayons for each table, and have the families decorate their labyrinth. When finished, it can be pasted onto the block of wood. Next, have each family member apply several coats of decoupage glue (available in a craft store) on top of the labyrinth pattern to seal the design to the wood. Families can then take their miniature labyrinths home to dry.

Encourage each family member to use their labyrinth throughout Lent for quiet prayer and reflection by using their fingers to "walk" the path of the labyrinth.

Hunger walk

There are various agencies today that sponsor walks to raise money to fight hunger. You can contact your diocese or town government to see if they do a walk for hunger. If so, the parish can work with them. If not, you may need to contact a national group, such as Bread for the World, to sponsor a local walk. You could also organize your own walk that might help establish a local food pantry or supply a soup kitchen, if there is no such service in your area.

The families can work as teams to accomplish different tasks necessary to put on a successful walk. Several families might get together to design and make a banner to be used as a welcome for the walkers. Other families might work on posters that can be carried during the walk, while others could inflate some balloons to be used as markers along the route. Other tasks to consider are sign-ups, sponsor forms, and providing refreshments for the workers and the walkers.

Many of the families will enjoy participating in the walk together. This is also an excellent way to involve both the greater community and neighboring parishes in an outreach project.

Butterfly house

This is another project that can be done during Lent in which the whole parish is involved, whether or not they directly participate.

To start, have a group of families construct a "butterfly house" that will fit into the gathering area of the church (preferably an area that does not get too cold). At our parish, we used a simple wooden frame that was 5' x 5' x 5' and lined the bottom with a vinyl tablecloth, stapling it to the frame. We then stapled colored netting (available at any sewing store) all around and on top of the frame. We added a green grass-like border at the bottom and a blue sky-type border at the top (you can get these borders from school supply companies).

About three or four weeks before Easter, each student is given a tiny caterpillar. (We ordered ours from Insect Lore, 132 S. Beech Street, Shafter, CA 93263, 1-800-LIVE-BUG.) The caterpillar comes in a tiny cup with its own food. We then put all the children's cups inside the butterfly house and add some bare twigs and branches.

The caterpillars eat and gradually get bigger. They start to crawl up the branches and spin their cocoons. Everyone waits and watches during the weeks of this process. If you plan it right—with help from Mother Nature, the insect supply company, and the goodness of God!—by Good Friday, the butterflies will start to emerge. You can add fresh flower branches to the butterfly house at this point. By Easter morning, you should have a beautiful house full of live butterflies!

The butterflies can be released outside after the Easter octave.

Of Related Interest...

Family Prayer for Family Times
Traditions, Celebrations, and Rituals
Kathleen O'Connell Chesto

Emphasizes the importance of establishing and maintaining prayer traditions in the home by offering general guidelines, specific examples, and complete prayer rituals for everyday and special occasions.   0-89622-668-9, 144 pp, $9.95 (M-53)

Make Family Time Prime Time
Fun Ways to Build Faith in Your Family
Denise Yribarren & DeAnn Koestner

Easy to duplicate ideas, activities, games, crafts, recipes, and rituals for holy days and holidays as well as for the everyday, mundane times.
0-89622-712-X, 112 pp, $12.95 (B-32)

Great for the RCIC!
Celebrating Catholic Rites and Rituals in Religion Class
Kathy Chateau and Paula Miller

By focusing on the liturgical experiences of children within the Catholic tradition, each chapter offers an introduction, directions for teachers, music suggestions, a prayer ritual, and suggestions for uses. Sample services focus on signing the senses with a cross, presentations of the creed and Bible, and a penitential rite.
0-89622-939-4, 80 pp, $12.95 (J-01)

Advent & Lent Activities for Children
Camels, Carols, Crosses, and Crowns
Shiela Kielly & Sheila Geraghty

Here's everything teachers, catechists, and parents ever wanted to know about Advent and Lent customs and traditions, as well as suggestions for sharing this information with children.   0-89622-676-X, 128 pp, $9.95 (M-51)

Available at religious bookstores or from:

TWENTY-THIRD PUBLICATIONS
A Division of Bayard PO BOX 180 · MYSTIC, CT 06355
1-800-321-0411 · FAX: 1-800-572-0788 · E-MAIL: ttpubs@aol.com
www.twentythirdpublications.com

Call for a free catalog